ADVANCE PRAISE

"Filled with powerful clinical vignettes and carefully articulated summaries of the science of parent–child relationships, this gem of a book will be useful for mental health practitioners and caregivers alike. Dan Hughes and Ben Gurney-Smith have created a wonderful compilation to ground the reader in the science and art of attachment that is sure to help the lives of the many children whose adults that care for them have the good sense and opportunity to read this life-affirming guide to love and connection."

—**Daniel J. Siegel,** M.D., New York Times bestselling author, *Aware: The Science and Practice of Presence*; and co-author, *The Power of Showing Up: How Parental Presence Shapes Who Our Kids Become and How Their Brains Get Wired*

"Taking us right into the heart of direct work, this book is a masterful exposition of Dan Hughes's hugely influential DDP model. Hughes is a veritable master in this field, and the text is informative, well-written, and brought alive by moving case examples. Integrating deep clinical experience with attachment theory, neurobiology, and intersubjectively infused developmental psychology, this book is a must-read for professionals working with children from complex backgrounds, and indeed, anyone interested in this area."

—**Graham Music,** Ph.D., Consultant Psychotherapist, Tavistock Clinic London, author of *Nurturing Natures, The Good Life,* and *Nurturing Children*

"It was a treat to read *The Little Book of Attachment* by Daniel Hughes and Ben Gurney-Smith! The authors identify three salient issues in treating children (safety, emotional regulation, and social cognition) and utilize Dyadic Developmental Psychotherapy to chart a course in working with parents and their children. A truly systemic and relational approach, this book describes how therapists can create safety, understand and get to know their clients, and create an environment of collaboration in which parents and children can co-regulate and synchronize their experiences with positive outcomes. Lovely, grounded, useful book!"

—**Eliana Gil, Ph.D.,** RPT-S, Senior Clinical and Research Consultant at Gil Institute for Tra Fairfax. VA

the little book
of attachment

A Norton Professional Book

the little book
of attachment

*Theory to Practice in Child Mental Health with
Dyadic Developmental Psychotherapy*

DANIEL HUGHES
BEN GURNEY-SMITH

W. W. NORTON & COMPANY
Independent Publishers Since 1923

Copyright © 2020 by Daniel A. Hughes and Ben Gurney-Smith

All rights reserved
Printed in the United States of America
First Edition

For information about permission to reproduce selections from this book, write to Permissions, W. W. Norton & Company, Inc., 500 Fifth Avenue, New York, NY 10110

For information about special discounts for bulk purchases, please contact W. W. Norton Special Sales at specialsales@wwnorton.com or 800-233-4830

Manufacturing by LSC Harrisonburg
Production manager: Katelyn MacKenzie

Library of Congress Cataloging-in-Publication Data

Names: Hughes, Daniel A., author. | Gurney-Smith, Ben, author.
Title: The little book of attachment : theory to practice in child mental health / Daniel A. Hughes and Ben Gurney-Smith.
Description: First edition. | New York : W. W. Norton & Company, [2020] | Series: A norton professional book | Includes bibliographical references and index.
Identifiers: LCCN 2019047650 | ISBN 9780393714357 (paperback) | ISBN 9780393714364 (epub)
Subjects: LCSH: Attachment disorder in children—Treatment. | Parent and child. | Child psychology.
Classification: LCC RJ507.A77 H85 2020 | DDC 618.92/8588—dc23
LC record available at https://lccn.loc.gov/2019047650

W. W. Norton & Company, Inc., 500 Fifth Avenue, New York, N.Y. 10110
www.wwnorton.com

W. W. Norton & Company Ltd., 15 Carlisle Street, London W1D 3BS

1 2 3 4 5 6 7 8 9 0

I would like to dedicate this book to Charlie, Toby, Rose, Megan, & Johnny and in memory of dear Boomer.

—Ben

I would like to dedicate this book to my most wonderful friend, Jon Baylin, whose vast knowledge about the human brain and heart has amazed and inspired me over and over again.

—Dan

contents

acknowledgments

I would firstly like to thank Dan, my coauthor, for his invitation to write with him. Dan: as someone who began to read your books and hear you speak many years ago, it has been such a privilege to work alongside you. Your ideas have been so instrumental to what I do today and have shaped me and many, many others.

Thanks, Kim Golding. As my supervisor and mentor you have been ever present, quiet yet sharp, and influential as my "secure base" in work. My deep thanks also to Jon Baylin. You have not only made laugh, but you have really helped my thinking on many occasions about the parenting brain "two step": *"thanks Doc!"*

I would like to recognize the people and the services which have shaped my understanding and practice to date: Adoptionplus (but especially Joanne Alper), the team at Clover Childcare Services (but especially Dan Knight and Kath Laidlaw), and my former colleagues at the ATTACH team and CAMHS in Oxford. All these have been innovative places to be. I am proud of what we have achieved together and what we have yet to do. My thanks and gratitude also to all the families I have met who—through some twist of fate—ended up with me sat before them and who have taught the greatest lessons.

To those really smart people who know their field and who gave helpful comments on earlier drafts: Helen Minnis, Kim Golding, Jess Christopher, and Charlie Gurney-Smith; thanks for helping me check out my reasoning when you probably had many other better things to do.

In a book principally about the value of relationships, it would be remiss not to give heartfelt recognition to those I love for their part in shaping me over the years. To my Mum and Dad, Margaret and Francis, I am grateful for the opportunities and freedoms you laid out for me growing up. Thanks Dad for the "common dog" (maybe I've earned those stripes now!). Thanks Mum, for the combination of the science and the arts. All these qualities are never far from what I do. To my sister Helen, whose great work in marine biology and climate change is literally the other side of the world, I'm glad and proud of what you are doing. To my closest friends Adam, Adrian, Ian, James, Jason, Kieran, Kristan, Marcus, and Richard, thank you for the constant source of brotherhood. To my children, Toby, Rose, Megan, and Johnny: keep on, keeping on! I will be there learning with you as we go along. And most emphatically in this series of deep gratitude to those I love, I would like to thank Charlie, my wife. When we first chartered our dreams, we would never have believed how far it would actually take us. In so many ways, I do not think I would be sitting here without you; thank you.

—BGS

I would like to acknowledge the many, many researchers over the past 70 years who have led us to understand how important attachment relationships are in our lives from the cradle to the grave. My great hope is that the therapeutic principles and interventions that we have presented here are consistent with the findings of this research.

I would also like to acknowledge the many professionals who are now members of the DDP community throughout the world, whose knowledge and sensitivities have greatly contributed to this model of therapy that is applying these important findings of attachment theory and research into our human endeavors.

Finally, I would like to acknowledge the significant contributions of my coauthor, Ben, to the writing of this book. Ben's knowledge of attachment research, his thorough and analytical mind as well as his compassionate heart, have been central in whatever contributions this book will make to utilizing attachment principles throughout the therapeutic community.

—DH

introduction

As child mental health professionals, we are familiar with the various presentations we see throughout our work week. As well-meaning individuals, we are likely to have equally varying motivations in the science and practice of our work. Some of these motivations will probably combine the professional and the personal. Our interests and areas of specialty may differ, too. Some of us may be motivated to develop a deeper working knowledge of behavioral presentations of conduct disorder, others will take an interest in the anxious or the depressed. Yet among this array of differences, there are some "universals" that are likely to have relevance to daily clinical practice and that we strive to address, in part, in this book. We have identified three such universals to set the scene for why the attachment-informed approach described in this book may have a wide appeal to child mental health professionals, whatever their background or trainings.

UNIVERSAL ONE:
PEOPLE MAKE JUDGMENTS QUICKLY

Wampold (2015) summarizes research that helps us understand why the first moments between client and therapist are so critical. Clinicians no doubt have experience with how important these first moments are. If we know that people make judgments about someone's trustworthiness (how safe they are) within 100 m/s and that clients are more likely to disengage after the first session than at any other stage of the therapy, it is worthwhile to pay attention to the therapeutic relationship from the very beginning, and maybe even before. For more reactive and mistrusting children and their parents, the likelihood of a move away from us (and therapy) is higher. What happens in these early moments helps set the foundation for trust building and exploration, which are, in themselves, key aspects of secure attachment relationships. In this book, we describe how an attachment-informed model of therapy pays particular attention to relational safety to facilitate trust, especially where attachment insecurity is present. The model we refer to in the book is Dyadic Developmental Psychotherapy (DDP). DDP is one example of a therapeutic approach which applies attachment theory to practice.

UNIVERSAL TWO:
OUTCOMES DEPEND ON
RELATIONSHIPS

A wealth of sound evidence reminds us that the human elements of relationships in therapy probably account for more variance in outcomes than the particular therapy or treatment model we adopt (Norcross & Wampold, 2018). These include demonstrably effective therapist qualities and behaviors, such as fostering the therapeutic alliance, collaboration, goal consensus, empathy, positive regard, and affirmation; and those behaviors that are classified as generally effective include repairing therapeutic ruptures and emotional expression (Wampold, 2015; Norcross & Wampold, 2018). We have previously reported on how many of these qualities, which are important to address in therapists regardless of their therapeutic orientation (Norcross & Wampold, 2018), relate to the fundamental aspects of DDP (Hughes, Golding, & Hudson, 2015, 2019). This affirmation of the importance of the therapeutic relationship is not necessarily new, but it supports the practice of DDP as a model, which values these relational qualities and behaviors in the interests of the client. As a book on attachment and its application to therapeutic practice, we describe how attachment theory and developmental theory informs the approach to moment-to-moment interactions with clients. How we embed these within our practice is described in this book, using examples from our clinical work.

UNIVERSAL THREE: RELATIONSHIPS NEED REPAIR

Once an engagement has been made, how open our clients are to our help, treatment, education, and guidance will determine much of our effectiveness in fulfilling our role and meeting their needs. It will also determine how satisfied they may be with our service and probably how rewarding we will find our work. For some children, attaining this kind of influence may be harder won. They may be suspicious, defensive, emotionally dysregulated at times, and even hostile to the well-intentioned helping hand we offer. Their history of relationships has taught them to be so. We, too, at times, may react defensively and in a closed way in these interactions. This may lead to moments of misunderstanding or misattunement. When we act on our misunderstandings, we rupture the relationship with our client. But we can take heart if we acknowledge that ruptures occur in all relationships; the seminal research conducted by Ed Tronick (2007) not only shows that such ruptures are always present between parent and infant, but also that how they are responded to—or not—is critical to the development of the child. From this detailed research, we learn that it is whether these ruptures are noticed and appropriate is action taken to repair the mistake that is crucial. So universal are these findings that Tronick's work has also been applied to the practice of psychotherapy (Stern et al., 1998), and rupture repair research is an important avenue in understanding effective therapies and therapists. In this way, how we attend to and repair these ruptures as they occur in our offices and clinics, through an open and engaged stance with our clients, not only reflects the evidence of effective therapists (Norcross & Wampold, 2018) but also embodies the authentic stance of DDP as a relational and attachment informed intervention. In this book, we describe how relationship repair is a critical component in an attachment lens and how this is addressed in the therapy.

This book is for all child and family mental health professionals who are interested in how attending to these universals using an attachment theory–informed therapeutic model can enhance their thinking, reasoning, and work to help build resilience in their clients and improve their clients' well-being.

HOW TO USE THIS BOOK

We have titled this book *The Little Book of Attachment* for a reason: We hope to make the application of attachment theory, which has led to profound and wide developments in child welfare policy, clinical practice, and research, accessible and practicable to child mental health professionals. DDP is the model of therapy put forward in this book, which applies this theory "in the moment" to clinical work with children and families. It is not only for situations in which attachment difficulty or insecurity are present, because establishing safety and trust, regulation, and reflection are critical to all work in human relationships and mental health. Nor is it limited to cases where maltreatment has been a feature (as we shall see this is not always synonymous with attachment insecurity). Therapists of children and families in mental health services will see children who have different histories and different patterns of attachment experiences. This book seeks to make the application of an attachment-informed model of therapy accessible in child and family mental health settings. We hope to demystify what it means to use attachment theory in practice.

This book begins with an overview of attachment theory set in the context of a therapy session before moving into a more referenced chapter that discusses the research linking attachment security with development and mental health. This points to a triad of developmental outcomes associated with attachment and disorder, which are the areas addressed by attachment-informed models of therapy. We then cover the core components of DDP and how they seek to build resilience by actively engaging with the triad of features associated with attachment and mental health disorders. Next, we "meet the parents" and describe the relevance of the parent's readiness for relationships in DDP. With this somewhat heavier work done, we invite the reader to witness more examples of the model through stories and dialogue with children and/or parents. The examples illustrate how DDP addresses the core elements found in mental health problems, including emotional regulation, reflective functioning, and trust in others, and how it helps develop coherent autobiographical memories and narratives. We hope the examples bring to life the implementation of an attachment perspective in a light, experiential, immersive, and practical way. In this manner, we invite the reader to incorporate the same open and engaged curiosity to the dialogue they have with their clients. An understanding through experience becomes more possible. Thinking *and* feeling are encouraged and with that, a known and felt sense of the approach may be more possible. Of course, we know that much of what is relevant and what makes something an experience is not communicated solely through words. Much may be happening beneath the waves of words, including affect, physiology, movement, social engagement, and so forth. We acknowledge this potential short coming as a feature of the written word. However, we have sought to convey the nuances of dialogue, using pauses, spaces, capital letters, and descriptions of emotion from both client and therapist, to cue the reader to some of the affective components that are so relevant in clinical work. Indeed, if told well, the narrative will affect the emotions of the reader and also give clues as to the experiences that occurred in the room. When working well, the dialogue between clinician and client will seem easygoing, almost conversational. It may be the absence of some of our usual instincts to ask direct questions or to move to reassurance or problem solving immediately that marks out the dialogue as being attachment-informed.

We hope that, whilst listening to our voices in these excerpts, you find *your* voice, in *your* work. Stephen Porges's polyvagal theory (Porges, 2009) demonstrates how our own sense of safety is transmitted through our vagal nerve and can be seen by our clients through the subtle alterations in the muscles around our eyes and in the musicality of our voices. How you embed the treatment interventions at your disposal, informed by the contents of this book, may depend on many things, including your felt sense of safety. We know, from our own experience of working with many children and parents, that families do best when they experience the therapist as authentic and genuine; comfortable in our own skin. In this book we discuss how this authenticity and comfort fosters trust, engagement, and openness to the ideas we cocreate to alleviate distress and build resilience. This position of mutual safety is a privileged position, and we treat this respectfully. We hope you perceive the authenticity of the dialogues we include, even as identifying information in examples about our clients has been changed to protect their privacy.

The terms used in attachment research and practice have been subject to change over the sixty or so years since John Bowlby, the father of attachment theory, highlighted the importance of a universal need for relationships. These changes were inevitable as the work expanded and deepened. But it does mean that terms like *reflective function* are synonymous with the newer term *mentalization*. Indeed, Dan Hughes, the first author of this book, who has published widely in this area of therapy over the years, has used terms such as reflective functioning in his previous books, and we tend to use this term here. However, we do refer to mentalization in the as used in the research we review and may use the term *to mentalize* to demonstrate the process of reflective functioning. In the research, *social cognition* encompasses a range of capacities for emotional understanding, recognition, views of the social world, trust, but also reflective functioning and mentalization. We group these capacities under the term social cognition when we discuss the research, and later in the book we may use social cognition as shorthand for many of the capacities for relationships. Emotional regulation incorporates physiological measures of emotional states, but it is also part of the executive functions. New models and theories have also taken a seat at the attachment table, such as polyvagal theory, and more recently, *blocked care.* The variations in terms and developments can be bewildering. So, because this is a book on applying attachment theory to mental health, we have tried to be clear about the terms we are using as we introduce them without losing their meanings or reference points along the way.

In seeking to be helpful to you, we make some assumptions about your practice. If you are a practicing clinician, we assume that you and your practice are safe, supervised, and informed by standardized and comprehensive assessments. This will lead to formulations of what is maintaining your clients' difficulties. We also assume you are able to recognize when a child's welfare and safety are in jeopardy and know when to enlist the cooperation of fellow agencies. Well-trained clinicians know that little can be achieved for the safety and benefit of the family without these cornerstones. How you approach the application of an attachment-informed model in detail will depend on your unique service and practice parameters. Our objective is to help you create safety in relational terms, having all these practice considerations already in place.

We invite you to make some assumptions about us, too. First, in our practice of DDP outlined in this book, we do not formally categorize parents and children using attachment classifications. Often the availability of the "gold standard" laboratory measures of attachment (and their trainings) are beyond what is feasible in child mental health settings. The Strange Situation (Ainsworth, Blehar, & Waters, 1978), for example, requires a video facility and the time to structure, administer, and then analyze according to the standards of this assessment. The same high standards of administration, reliability checks, and analysis apply for the Childhood Attachment Interview (Target, Fonagy, & Shmueli-Goetz, 2003) and the Adult Attachment Interview (George, Kaplan, & Main, 1996). Adherence to these standards is vital if we are to have confidence in the findings of research using attachment theory. However, although they may be used in practice, in this book it is not essential to explicitly make these classifications, for two reasons. Firstly, the context is focusing on child mental health problems, not attachment difficulties per se. Secondly, as an attachment theory–informed model of practice, DDP focuses attention on those developmental features associated with secure attachment—namely emotional regulation and capabilities we refer to as social cognition—which are often low in children with mental health difficulties. The rationale for DDP as an attachment-based model applied to child mental health is that we are able to develop these areas of resilience through the provision of features of secure attachment relationships to both the parent and child. Attachment security may indeed change during therapy, and research is needed to investigate this, but in essence, the focus is on creating safe, reciprocal relationships as well as on enhancing regulation and reflection/ social cognition, which are important factors associated with mental health. Focusing on developing these features of mental health rather than developing a secure attachment classification will seem a less onerous and more familiar therapeutic goal to mental health practitioners.

Second, although we refer to the DDP model, and there is some evidence of its effectiveness as a method of parenting and psychotherapy (see Hughes et al., 2015, 2019), we do not describe the DDP model as the only way. There are certainly other well-respected and also evidence-based approaches to addressing attachment difficulties and mental health disorders. We also recognize the importance of psychopharmacological interventions in addressing mental health disorders. We know that whilst the research foundation for the model of DDP is strong, as described in this book, we need to build on the present evidence for the effectiveness of DDP as a psychotherapy (e.g., Hughes, Golding & Hudson, 2015, 2019). Important work is underway to investigate this robustly and with the kind of rigour which meaningfully contributes to the evidence base for children and families. We propose that clinicians who are trained in a range of treatment models, such as social learning theory, cognitive behavioral therapy, or others, may benefit from the model described in this book, as it will enhance their engagement, connection, and practice with children and families. In essence, a relational approach may increase the likelihood that the treatment models you use will be relevant to the family. We do not suggest one model over the other, but instead see and describe the benefit of integrating DDP—an attachment perspective—to inform one's practice, whatever treatment model is adopted.

With all this in mind, we hope this book is helpful in enhancing the human and relational endeavor of your practice as a child and family mental health professional.

the little book
of attachment

chapter one

An Attachment Perspective

We begin by sharing this therapeutic session to set the stage for the attachment perspective that is the organizing principle for this book. Since attachment involves unique relationships between parent and child, we chose an example with two parents and their child to illustrate the implications of using attachment theory as the template for the therapeutic approach.

ONE THERAPEUTIC SESSION

Rachel is a family therapist who utilizes the principles of attachment in her therapy. This example session was her third session with Sarah and Jon, the parents of Michael, age 12. It was the first session in which Michael joined them. It begins with her finishing up her conversation with Michael about his trip down the coast with his friend Stan and Stan's family on Saturday.

RACHEL: Well, Michael, sounds as if you had a great time. If we meet again, I'd love to see that giant light blue shell that you found.

MICHAEL: Yeah, I guess.

RACHEL: [Continuing with her relaxed, rhythmic voice] Thanks. And I'm glad that it was such a good day for you. I heard that Sunday seemed like it was a lot harder, when you and your parents had an argument over your plans for this coming weekend. What was that about?

MICHAEL: [With some intensity] I have to spend more time with the family! That's what they always say! It's not like we have a good time or anything! We either fight or we're all bored.

RACHEL: [Leaning forward in her chair and matching his intensity with her voice] Ah, so this has happened before, too! It seems to you that your parents want to spend more free time with you than you want to spend with them.

MICHAEL: It's not that they LIKE to spend time with me. They HAVE TO. That's their job if they're going to be "family of the year" on our street!

RACHEL: So it seems to you that they don't really enjoy being with you. It seems more like they want to impress the neighbors, not really be with you. It doesn't sound like you feel very close to them.

MICHAEL: [Still speaking with anger, though with a tinge of regret] Why would I! Melanie [Michael's 15-year-old sister] is the good one. They like being with her and they're stuck with me.

RACHEL: [Responding with a light, gentle, reflective tone] Ah,

Michael. So, it seems to you that your parents are closer to your sister than to you. Like in your family, you're the odd-man-out.

MICHAEL: [Quietly, with no anger now, only resignation and a hint of sadness] I am. It seems like I'm never good enough for them.

RACHEL: [Even more quietly] Ah, Michael. You feel that your parents are disappointed in you. How hard that must be if it seems that way to you! How hard.

Now the four of them sat quietly for a moment before Rachel continued to develop the conversation around themes of isolation and shame—realities for Michael that were seldom seen because they were hidden under his anger. Sarah and Jon sat quietly, with some anxiety and confusion over Michael's words. They wanted to speak but had agreed with Rachel that they would not respond to Michael until Rachel asked them to do so. Rachel had said that her first goal would be to help Michael to express his experience of the events that were happening in their home, and she would hear their experiences later. She would invite them to speak with Michael after she had helped him to become vulnerable with her and after they all understood his experience. And then—with her guidance—Sarah and Jon could respond with understanding and empathy for how things seemed to him.

SARAH AND JON'S FIRST SESSION— EARLY EXPERIENCES

In the two earlier sessions, when she met with Sarah and Jon without Michael, Rachel was able to get an understanding of their perspective of the struggles that they were and had been having with Michael for quite some time.

They spoke in detail about how they worried about his anger, his indifference to whatever family activity they planned, his long hours in his room, and his shutting down when they asked him what was bothering him. They acknowledged that these worries were not new, only greater. Even during his preschool years Michael was quick to become angry and seemed to misbehave again and again, even when it was clear that he knew what he was supposed to be doing and it was obvious that he would receive a consequence for what he did wrong. Consequences only made him more angry. Now Michael, who had recently turned 12, was becoming more defiant, saying that he did not have to do what they wanted him to do and that they could not make him. If he wanted to visit a friend and was told no, he would scream that they hated him. And his harsh words never ended: "You only care about what you want; what I want is not important to you!" "I'd rather have any other parents than you!" "You only care about Melanie!" Rachel learned that when Sarah and Jon had consulted with a mental health professional in the past, they were told that their son most likely was developing an oppositional-defiant disorder.

As Sarah and Jon spoke, Rachel tried to understand how their relationship with Michael was affecting them and the whole family. She expressed empathy with how hard it seemed to be for them.

Sarah reacted quickly and strongly, "Well it would be hard for you, too! What do you think it's like to have your child scream at you and say that you're a terrible parent! Of course it's hard!"

Rachel leaned forward and replied with similar intensity in her tone but without the defensiveness expressed by Sarah. "I'm sorry, Sarah, that I said that in a way that led you to experience me as being critical of you. It may have seemed to you that I thought you should not be upset over the struggles you are having with Michael and with the intensity of his anger toward you."

Rachel's clear acceptance of Sarah's experience caused an immediate change in her response to Rachel. Sarah replied in a way that showed how exhausted and discouraged she was. "I don't understand why he never seems to be happy with the life we are giving him. We try so hard to be good parents and yet it is never enough. He is always disappointed in us!"

"I can see that, Sarah; I can see how hard you are trying to give Michael a good home and to have a close, loving relationship with him."

Sarah interrupted Rachel and said, "I'm not good enough for him! Why is he never satisfied with who I am?"

Gently, Rachael asked, "When is it the hardest for you?"

Sarah stared at Rachel with pain and fear in her eyes, "When he screams at me. I hear hate in his voice, and I see it in his eyes." Sarah began to cry, and Jon reached over and held her hand.

"Has it felt that way for long?" Rachel asked.

"I first started feeling that way when he was only three or four. He always seemed to be unhappy. Nothing was good enough. Melanie had been such an easy baby to raise. She was a delight. Michael seemed more like a challenge. Sometimes even a burden." Sarah looked frightened when she said that, searching for disapproval in Rachel's face. When she could see only acceptance and empathy she continued.

"Actually, he may have been an actual burden and it wasn't his fault. I was depressed for many months after his birth. Sometimes I didn't have any energy and could not go to him when he was crying. Jon was having some work problems then and he just didn't seem to understand how hard it was for me to get anything done. So he and I would argue—something we had hardly ever done before—and then it was even harder to take care of Michael."

Jon joined the conversation. "That's how I see it too. I just didn't get how hard it was and I'd say that things were hard for me at work, too, and I just needed to relax some when I came home. Then I felt that either I just didn't know how to meet Sarah's needs or that her needs were excessive and she was asking too much. I'm not proud of how I was back then but I think—I hope—it's not affecting our relationship now. Sarah smiled and squeezed his hand to confirm that she agreed.

Rachel asked, "Did Michael cry much when he was a baby?"

"All the time and it drove me crazy! I could never make him happy. I know now that my depression was probably a big part of it—I did not respond quickly or well when he cried—but I did not think of that at the time. He just seemed to be too demanding." Sarah then paused and reflected for a moment. "And then he stopped crying. Of course that didn't bother me, it was a relief, he no longer was a burden."

"Did he seem happier then?" Rachel asked.

"I wouldn't go that far. It just seemed that—maybe about the time he started crawling—that he could get by on his own. He never seemed to be interested in doing things with me like Melanie was. And again, I just accepted that. Maybe with some relief."

Rachel gently continued the conversation about the early years with Michael. "Do you think that maybe some of his unhappiness and complaining started in those early years? At first because of your depression after giving birth, because you were not able to respond to his unhappiness. Then he stopped seeking comfort from you. He would manage things on his own. Yet, little kids can't manage things well on their own, so it seemed to him that things never did go well. And he did not know how to let himself be comforted by you. You may have tried to help him, but when it did not seem to help, you lost confidence and didn't try as much, leading him to think that you did not want to help him and leading you to think that he didn't want your help."

Sarah seemed shocked. As if things were beginning to make sense in a way that never had occurred to her before. A few examples came to mind along the lines of what Rachel had suggested. Jon added his perception that Michael did not want his support either. He would try to help Michael feel better, but it never seemed to work. After a while, he, too, tried less. It seemed to be easier than trying and failing, or worse yet, trying and being rejected.

The three of them reflected a bit more, and Rachel suggested that they meet one more time before asking Michael to join them again. Sarah and Jon agreed.

SARAH AND JON'S SECOND SESSION— EARLIER EXPERIENCES

In the next session Sarah and Jon were quick to continue their discussion with Rachel about those early years. They felt her understanding made sense, but they were confused about what they might do to change things. They worried that it might be too late—that what started when Michael was an infant would not be likely to change.

Rachel understood their worries and indicated that she'd have ideas about how to approach Michael with regard to those past events, but she first wanted to understand their history more fully. She turned to Sarah and asked her to describe more fully her experience of hearing hatred in Michael's voice and seeing it in his eyes when he was angry with her.

Sarah replied with some distress, "It's so hard when he is angry with me. It's like I'm not good enough for him—and I'll never be good enough! I feel that I'll never know what to do to make him just love me for who I am."

"Does anger often have that impact on you?" Rachel asked.

Sarah replied, "I don't like anger, I never did. When my parents were angry with each other, sometimes they didn't seem to talk with each other for days. When my mother was angry with me, I worried that she might not talk to me for days, even though she never did that."

"What was she likely to be angry about?" Rachel continued.

"It seemed like she was angry about anything and everything. Like I could never please her. Sometimes I thought that I just was not the daughter that she wanted." Sarah cried quietly as she remembered her experiences with her mother.

Rachel leaned closer to Sarah and quietly said, "How hard it must have been when you did not think that you were good enough to be your mother's daughter . . . and now how hard it is when you think that you are not good enough to be your son's mother."

Sarah looked into Rachel's caring eyes and then burst into tears. Jon held her. She looked at him and said as she cried, "I failed as a daughter and now I'm failing as a mother."

After Sarah spoke with Rachel some more about her sense of failing Michael, Jon looked to Rachael and said, "Sarah is not alone in this. My parents always seemed to be too busy for me. Sometimes I thought that if I were a better son, they would want to be with me more. I have the same feelings when my son does not want to spend time with me. I, too, feel that I'm failing as Michael's parent. And I always promised myself that I would be a better father than my father was with me."

Jon then gave some examples of hard times in his childhood when his parents were not available to him. Toward the end of the session, Rachel looked at them both and said, "You two have such courage to be willing to experience—again—much of the pain of your past in order to help your son and your relationship with him. What you are doing is so crucial if you and I are going to help him to experience again some of his early years in order to help him with his struggles in his life today."

"What can we do?" they both asked.

"Listen to his experience—so similar to your own—most likely that he is not good enough for you, that you wish that you had a different son, that he is a burden to you. Listen and do not defend yourself. Listen and do not explain. Listen and understand, and then feel his loneliness and anger and shame with him. That will be hard, and I will help you at every step of the way. I will help him to experience how special he is to you, how much you love him, and how sad you are that he has these experiences. And together we will help him to experience your love, your comfort, and your unconditional acceptance of who he is. If you want me to."

"Yes, yes, yes!" they both exclaimed.

"I knew you would want me to. Let me help you to anticipate how our next sessions with Michael are likely to go and what I will be asking of you. I'll help you to find the words that he needs to hear from you, that you may not have spoken."

"Let's begin now!" Sarah said. Jon agreed. And they did.

Patterns of attachment pass down through generations. Therapy based on attachment principles begins with understanding the current troubles within the context of the child's attachment with their parents. From there, the therapist searches for the development and expression of these patterns from the child's birth through the present. Once the child's attachment patterns that are seen in the family's daily life are understood, the therapist strives to understand the parents' attachment patterns that originated in their childhoods. There are likely to be connections between the parents' attachment styles and those of their child. Understanding these connections will enable the therapist—along with the parents and child—develop a way forward that addresses the attachment-based components of the presenting problems. This new knowledge is likely to reduce the shame associated with the current functioning of both the child and the child's parents, while offering ways to improve the emotional, reflective, and relationship skills of the whole family.

ATTACHMENT THEORY

At its core, attachment theory focuses on how the young child learns to regulate his distress by relying on his parents. In secure attachment relationships, the young child strives to stay near enough to his parents that they can assist him with any distress and become safe again. When safe, he is able to develop his own somewhat independent interests and skills, much of which also occurs through the active presence of his parents (secure pattern). Sometimes it does not go as the child had planned, as happens when his parents are seldom available or not available consistently enough to ensure that his distress will be regulated and he can develop his interests and skills. In this case, the child needs to develop his own resources to try to manage distress. He may avoid relying on his parents, learning to "go-it-alone" (avoidant pattern). Or he may search for ways to control his parents, continuously inducing them to try handle his distress by keeping them close through constant signals of dependency (anxious/ambivalent pattern). These children at best devote most of their resources to developing some ability to regulate their distress. In the worse cases, children are overwhelmed with distress; often their parent is either the source of the distress or is unable to resolve it. This then manifests in many symptoms of dysregulated cognitive, emotional, and behavioral functioning (disorganized pattern).

It has been fifty years since John Bowlby wrote his three-volume set *Attachment and Loss*. His theory stimulated an extensive body of research that has created a dominant, organizing foundation for understanding major aspects of human development. Early research by Mary Ainsworth and others on these developing patterns of attachment, identified three patterns—avoidant (A), secure (B), and anxious/ambivalent (C). The fourth pattern, explored in depth a few decades later by Mary Main and others, was called disorganized (D). The disorganized pattern is considered to pose the greatest risk for mental health problems, though both avoidant and anxious/ambivalent also are associated with some risk factors. Mary Main also was at the forefront of many researchers who determined that the parents' attachment histories played a strong causative role in their child's attachment patterns (Hesse, 2016). Interventions to influence the development of children's attachment patterns increasingly included interventions that addressed the attachment patterns of their parents. There are times when stressors in the parents' current life make it very difficult for them to respond to their child's attachment behaviors that reflect a need for parental care; we have identified this process as *blocked care* (Hughes & Baylin, 2012, which is discussed in detail in Chapter 4). DDP takes a family perspective to understand and provide interventions for emotional and behavioral problems that have an attachment-related component.

Attachment theory and research have found an important place in the fields of infant and child development, education, social services, health, and mental health. This book focuses on the impact of attachment on mental health, specifically the value of attachment theory and research for therapeutic efforts to facilitate the mental health of vulnerable children.

A central feature of attachment theory is the demonstration of the various regulatory systems that a young child develops to handle distress. Distinct patterns of behavior in the child's attachment relationships reflect the relative success or failure of this quest. It is no wonder that these attachment relationships

gradually became the focus of a great deal of efforts to understand the developmental needs of young children. This focus
originated in London, England, where John Bowlby studied
and practiced during World War II. This was a time that was
replete with separation and loss for children associated with the
war; they were evacuated and separated from their parents with
the prospect of potential losses of parents being killed at home
or abroad. In addition to his service in the military working
with war effected veterans, John Bowlby spent time working at
a school for maladjusted children. This was a formative time in
the genesis of attachment theory. It was there that he made key
observations of how early experience might account for certain
later difficulties in children, linking early loss with behavioral
difficulties. John Bowlby's unique training, both as a doctor
and analyst, combined an understanding of the biological with
the psychological. This rich vein still runs through attachment
theory and research today.

This book describes Dyadic Developmental Psychotherapy
(DDP) in some detail. DDP is one model of therapy that applies
attachment theory principles and interventions to foster qualities in
the child's development that have been shown to be enhanced by
a secure attachment. These abilities include emotional regulation,
reflective function, an internal working model of self and other,
reciprocal conversational and relational skills, the ability to repair
important relationships following conflict, and the development of
a coherent autobiographical narrative. Since attachment is a very
complex and fertile model for understanding development, there
are many models of psychotherapy based on attachment principles.
We have chosen to describe the connection between attachment
and DDP based on the research linking attachment with development and mental health that we will outline in Chapter 2.

Attachment theory and research focus on the nature of the
child's relationship with her parent or caregiver as well as the effect

of this relationship on the child's development and well-being. The attachment relationship is a highly specific affective bond between child and parent, a bond that is distinct from other affective bonds in that its primary function is to ensure the child's safety. Within this safe space, the child relies on her parent for support and guidance in becoming successful in her major developmental tasks. When children are safe with their parents, they are likely to trust them to meet their ongoing physical and psychological needs. When a child is able to trust her parent, that child is likely to be able to regulate her emotions when near her parent, initially through the experience of the parent coregulating her emotional states. When she is able to trust her parent, she is also able to rely on her parent to help her make sense of what is happening, and through repetition, she will develop reflective functioning.

Attachment principles can influence the nature of psychotherapy most directly when attachment theory is used as a guide for developing the therapeutic relationship. The principles that enable a secure attachment with the parent to facilitate the child's safe development at home are also the principles that enable the therapeutic relationship to facilitate the child's development of desirable mental health qualities within psychotherapy. DDP goes further, in that this model of attachment-based therapy aims to facilitate both the features of a secure attachment in the child's relationship with the therapist, as well as the parent's ability to enable the child to demonstrate these same qualities in the parent–child relationship at home. In DDP, the qualities of trust, emotional regulation, and reflective functioning tend to be continuously maintained and enhanced.

THE PARENT–CHILD RELATIONSHIP

Attachment behaviors are evident when the young child relies on her caregivers for safety from threats as well as for provisions, such as food and clothing, that enable her to survive. These parental behaviors to promote her survival will intensify whenever she is at risk. Her parents need to be available when she needs them! The better her parents are at identifying and providing what she needs to survive, and the more committed they are to doing what is in her best interest, the more likely she will be able to rely on herself when she reaches maturity.

As her parents are consistently available, sensitive to her expressions of need, and responsive to her, her trust in them increases. They will not hurt or abandon her. Rather they will act in what they believe to be in her *best* interest. She is learning to trust them! She trusts that they will do what they think is best for her, and that they consider what is best for her to be a very high priority in their lives. Attachment theory first focused on the parents providing for the child's immediate safety. Through having her moment-to-moment safety needs met, the child gradually came to trust that her parents would focus on ensuring her overall best interest. Her mind became organized around this trust in her parents, and her mind also began to conclude that their minds were focused on meeting her needs. These needs went beyond her immediate needs for safety. The child is a social being who needs to learn how to communicate and engage in complex reciprocal relationships with other people. Sharing socially relevant information is seen as another key function of attachment, in addition to the survival function referred by some as "epistemic trust" (we will discuss epistemic trust more in the next chapter). Her parents would relate with her in a way that models how she should relate with others—in a similar trusting, reciprocal manner. The child needs to regulate her emotional states and make sense of her intentions as well as those of her parents. Children will learn more from their parents and accept their guidance when they trust that their parent's intention is to do what is best for them, not to frustrate or hurt them. Children need to trust that even if they do something that their parents do not want them to do, their parents will continue to care for them—to know their relationship is more important than any conflicts or differences of opinion.

Children who are securely attached to their parents trust that their parents will be committed to what is best for them, including what is best for their emotional, social, cognitive, physical, and moral development. If children trust that these are their parents' dominant intentions toward them, they will experience a deep sense of safety, from which they will be more willing and able to explore the world and their place in the world. They will learn that they are able to trust other adults in addition to their parents. From this perspective, we may achieve better insight regarding how we might engage with children who are vulnerable with regard to various aspects of their development. We might see how the parent–child relationship, with its secure attachment, facilitates many key aspects of the child's development. We also might then see how the therapist takes knowledge derived from that relationship to guide the developing therapeutic relationship.

Let's explore now the many aspects of a child's development that are enhanced by a secure attachment to their parents.

THE DEVELOPMENT OF A SYNCHRONIZED RECIPROCAL RELATIONSHIP BETWEEN PARENT AND INFANT

When the child is physically and psychologically safe, he is open and engaged with his parent. The ongoing pattern of engagement with a sensitive and responsive parent creates more safety for the child! The parent is getting to know the child as the parent alternates their initiatives, which convey interest and delight, with responses to the child's communications about how he hopes to engage in that immediate moment. We will now share a number of quotes from John Bowlby, whose theory of human development generated so many of the ideas that are discussed in this book. Bowlby describes this synchronized pattern of relatedness very well:

> A sensitive mother regulates her behaviour so that it meshes with his. In addition, she modifies the form her behaviour takes to suit him: her voice is gentle but higher pitched than usual, her movements slowed, and each next action adjusted in from and timing according to how her baby is perform-ing. Thus she lets him call the tune and, by a skillful inter-weaving of her own responses with his, creates a dialogue. (Bowlby, 1988, p. 7)

Within this nonverbal pattern of engagement, the parent and infant continuously influence each other, alternating initiatives and responses, coming to know each other in their intentions, affective states, and interests. Knowing and being known are occurring simultaneously. The child is discovering that she is delightful, interesting, and lovable because her parent is com-municating those experiences of the child as she is engaging her. Let's again consider the words of Bowlby about this process:

> For a relationship between any two individuals to proceed harmoniously, each must be aware of the other's point of view, his goals, feelings, and intentions, and each must so adjust his own behaviour that some alignment of goals is negotiated. This requires that each should have reason-ably accurate models of self and other which are regularly up-dated by free communication between them. It is here that the mothers of the securely attached children excel

and those of the insecure are markedly deficient. (Bowlby, 1988, p. 131)

It is during those highly synchronized, nonverbal, *intersubjective* experiences between the parent and infant that the young child is learning to communicate with her parents. These experiences have been described by Daniel Stern (1985) and Colwyn Trevarthen, (2001))among others, as being intersubjective because the experiences are being jointly created within the interwoven subjective experiences of each. The infant is learning the art of engaging in conversations with her parents about her experiences and her parents' experiences. Bowlby also noted that

"long before the appearance of words, the pattern of turn-taking so characteristic of human conversation is already present." (1988, p. 8)

From the safety that comes from a secure attachment, children quickly become highly engaged in learning to have conversations with others! This is both a deeply enjoyable and interesting activity for infants and their parents, and it is the origin of the reciprocal conversations we have with others throughout our lives. Within these conversations, the child is developing a sense of who she is and who her parents are. Soon, the eyes of both parent and child turn outward to the world, and the infant learns to rely on the meanings they learned from their parents experience of the world as they begin to develop their own meanings.

These conversations between the securely attached young child and parent are characterized by a freedom to explore each other's points of view, conveying a sense of openness and interest in each other's perspectives that is not characteristic of children who are not securely attached to their parents (Bowlby, 1988).

What begin as delightfully reciprocal nonverbal communications between parent and infant continue and evolve as the child develops and integrates words into the dialogue. For the most part, the trend in the relationship is toward a strong, synchronized quality of conversation, with fluid turn-taking and congruent affective expressions, ensuring that both participants are interested in the discussion, while being ready to modify the thrust of the discussion as the wishes of one or both begin to change. The relationship between a securely attached child and his parents contains many such diverse, emotionally rich conversations throughout his childhood and adolescence. These conversations are quite elaborative and descriptive and bring complex psychological realities into the mind of the child. These conversations involve a cooperative negotiation of differences and tend to blend the autonomous needs of both parent and child while at the same time conveying a commitment to their relationship.

Children who are not securely attached tend to develop in the context of disturbed conversations with their parents. These conversations are considered to be disrupted, and they exhibit five distinct features: The parents tend to bring negative, intrusive content into the conversation. They place their interests above those of their children. These parents also convey confusing affective messages and do not respond to their child's cues for comfort. They show odd mannerisms in their voice prosody and gestures and postures with their child. These nonverbal expressions are not in sync with their words. Finally, they tend to hold back or withdraw from the child and not complete the conversation, being only partly engaged with their child. These five features are more predictive of dissociation and disorganized attachment than is child maltreatment (Lyons-Ruth & Jacobvitz, 2016).

Conversations that are open and reciprocal, conveying nonjudgmental interest in the experiences of the parent, child, and therapist—conversations that build trust—are the central tenet of DDP. Within these conversations, the child (and parent) are ensured safety and all experiences are welcomed. We will describe how the research supports the definition of security as being open to both positive and negative emotional states. Secure attachment does not discriminate. Insecurity probably does. Often a child with attachment challenges will have difficulty engaging in reciprocal conversations. The therapist will use the parent–infant synchronized reciprocal nonverbal communications as the template for the conversations that the therapist works to facilitate during treatment sessions. The content of the conversation is secondary to the process itself: helping children to learn how to engage in these give and take, nonverbal/verbal communications. While engaging in this process, children are supported in developing regulation as well as reflective functioning skills. As these skills develop, children begin to be able to have conversations about content that had been embedded in shame and fear. The child's engagement becomes intersubjective, and she is then open to new, integrative stories that heal and generate new meanings.

Yes, in therapy, stories begin to emerge within the conversations that the parent and child have about the events of their shared life. The events described in the conversations become organized into cohesive bits of meaning that form stories. These stories form a joint history, which in itself becomes an important aspect of the child's ongoing sense of safety within his home. Too often, when children and their parents are experiencing ongoing distress and psychological defensiveness in their relationships, the stories that they are developing tend to be incomplete and characterized by fear and shame.

The stories that develop in therapy are often stories that are characteristic of individuals who have secure attachment relationships. Securely attached children, if they maintain this classification during their developmental years, are classified as manifesting autonomous attachment as adults. These people are successful at maintaining a balance between relying on themselves and relying on others to meet their needs for safety. They have achieved a balance between their needs for individuation and their needs for reciprocal intimacy. To quote Bowlby (1988) once again:

> "If, in reviewing his attachment relationships during the course of psychotherapy and restructuring his working models, it is the emotional communications between a patient and his therapist that play the crucial part." (p. 157)

As the stories of securely attached children develop and become integrated during the course of the individual's life, they form what is described as a coherent autobiographical narrative—a characteristic of the autonomously attached adult. The life story of the autonomously attached adult is organized, comprehensive, consistent, and concise. The various events of the individual's life have become integrated, and the overall identity of the individual "makes sense." There are no parts of the individual's history that need to be split off because they are covered with shame or terror. The person lives his life now, in its entirety. The life of the autonomously attached adult is embedded in the safety inherent within his attachment classification. From this safety can be traced cycles of conversations, leading to stories, leading to this autobiographical narrative that is truly coherent. Such a narrative is a central feature of our mental health.

A BRIEF LOOK AT THE POLYVAGAL THEORY

Since Bowlby developed his ideas on relationships, there have been several advances in thinking and research in the realm of neurobiology that build on his work. We would like to take a quick look at a neurobiological theory that complements the attention that we are giving to attachment theory. For a more detailed look at how our entire neurological system functions best within the context of relationships as we are describing, we refer readers to *Brain-Based Parenting* (Hughes & Baylin, 2012), *The Neurobiology of Attachment-Focused Therapy* (Baylin & Hughes, 2016), and the second edition of *The Developing Mind* (Siegel, 2012).

Following his extensive studies of the autonomic nervous system, Stephen Porges developed the polyvagal theory (2009). Prior to Porges' research, we knew that the autonomic nervous system was comprised of the sympathetic (or mobilization) system and the parasympathetic (immobilization) system. Mental health practitioners became interested in the autonomic nervous system because of its role in keeping us safe, providing our defensive responses to threats. The sympathetic branch drew our attention first because it explained how we mobilize through aggression, fleeing, or maintaining a vigilant, frozen state in response to threats. Later we became interested in the role of the parasympathetic system in creating a dissociative, vegetative state of immobilization when both fight and flight are not effective or not possible.

But Porges noted that the parasympathetic system is also very active when we are feeling safe. The parasympathetic system has two branches: one mediated by the dorsal vagal nerves, activated by threat (leading to immobilization with fear), and one mediated by the ventral vagal nerves, activated when we are feeling safe (leading to immobilization without fear). Porges described the activity of the ventral vagal circuit as the social engagement system, which is crucial for the development of our survival skills if we are to thrive as social mammals. He highlighted the activity of the cranial nerves that are essential to our ability to receive and signal nonverbal cues that enable us to communicate important interpersonal experiences with each other. When the social engagement system is active, Porges states, we are in an "open and engaged" state of mind, in contrast to the defensive state of mind that is active when we are under threat.

It is this open and engaged state of mind that will be of interest to us throughout this work. In this state of mind, in which we are open to the experiences of another while being engaged with them in a reciprocal manner, our attachment-based relationships flourish. We will be describing how an open and engaged manner of relating is both a central goal of our attachment-based interventions as well as the means by which we are able to achieve them. The range of open and engaged interactions will be presented in more detail in Chapter 5.

REGULATING EMOTIONAL STATES

Attachment relationships contain significant emotional meanings for both members of the dyad. These meanings involve love and fear, sadness and joy, excitement and anger. When the parent and infant are engaged in reciprocal, attuned interactions in which they are communicating nonverbally with their facial expressions, voice prosody, gestures, touch, and timing, the emotional qualities of the experience quickly become synchronized. The affective expressions of the infant's emotions are coregulated by the parent's attuned response. The expressions of agitated distress made by the infant are matched with similar—though regulated—rhythms and degrees of intensity by the parent. In so doing, the infant's expressions are heard and understood. The parent is saying "I get it!" and the infant is saying, "You understand!" When the nonverbal communication is successful, the infant's emotions tend to become less intense.

The distress of the infant—if it is not met and understood

by a sensitive parent—tends to increase, and at some point it might well become dysregulated. Infants have little ability to regulate emotional states. These states might be painful, confusing, or frightening, and the infant's affective expressions of his emotions represent, in part, an effort to create a needed sense of safety by evoking a connection with his attachment figure. The affective engagement of the attachment figure—as long as it remains regulated—enables the infant to remain regulated. The parent's attuned presence enables the infant's emotional state to be coregulated. The parent is communicating "I understand your emotional state; I will be with you in this state so you will not have to handle it alone; and I will help you to understand its meaning so that it is not frightening to you." The infant cannot do this alone. The coregulation of his emotional states with the active, regulated engagement of his parent must precede his gradually developing ability to autoregulate such states.

Our ability to identify, regulate, and express our emotional life is very reflective of our attachment patterns. Children who have developed an avoidant attachment pattern find emotions to be very difficult to handle and they are likely to avoid emotional events, themes, and conversations. When their avoidant strategies are ineffective in dealing with an intense emotional experience, they are at risk of becoming dysregulated, with rageful outbursts, states of panic, or overwhelming despair. These states represent a failure of their primary, detached manner of coping with life, and they are likely to experience shame. Children with an anxious/ambivalent attachment pattern tend to be habitually on the edge of stressful emotional states, seeking relief from these states through their attachment figures but not finding comfort. Especially intense emotional experiences are also likely to place these children at risk of becoming dysregulated, as their anxious, dependent vigilance does not prove to be up to the task of creating a semblance of safety.

Both patterns make it difficult for the child to engage in reciprocal conversations about important emotional themes with an attachment figure. The avoidant child is likely to focus on facts, dwelling on facts that tend to bring some calm while avoiding others, and fail to develop a coherent story. The anxious/ambivalent child is likely to focus only on the emotional content of events and to fail to develop stories that make sense of the stressful events in their lives. The challenges faced by the avoidant child and the anxious child are likely to be relatively minor compared to those faced by the child with attachment disorganization. When under stress, these children are likely to be flooded with dysregulated emotions, falling into intense, impulsive behaviors and/or dissociative states. The securely attached child is able to engage in a wide range of conversations about emotional themes. Their memory for both positive and negative emotional experiences is more comprehensive than is the memory of children who are insecurely attached. Emotions add to the richness, satisfaction, and meaning in the lives of securely attached children. They are likely to bring joy to this child's life and do not require vigilant defensiveness or efforts to minimize their place in his life.

It is likely that Michael's functioning demonstrated qualities of an avoidant attachment pattern, in which he tended to avoid exploring emotional themes, resisted being comforted by his parents, and relied on himself more than on his parents. When he could not avoid stressful themes, he tended to react with intense anger toward his parents. His pattern may well have been activated by Sarah's depression in his early months, during which she was slow to respond to his distress with comfort. He also had difficulty regulating his anger because anger was difficult for both of his parents to coregulate, given their attachment histories.

DEVELOPING REFLECTIVE FUNCTIONING

A crucial developmental task for children is to develop their reflective functioning; an important part of what is termed *social cognition* in some of the research. Reflective functioning skills enable them to develop the ability to identify and express qualities of the inner lives of themselves and others (i.e., what they and others think, feel, value, want, intend, and perceive).

Securely attached children are not only able to communicate their intentions but they are also fairly accurate at reading the intentions of others. They develop an awareness that what they think and feel about behaviors or events may differ from what their parents think and feel about them. They—and their parents—are likely to be able to accept and openly explore these differences. The parents of securely attached children frequently engage in sensitive, empathic reading of the mind of their child while also making clear their own minds. These parents value conversations that are psychologically meaningful to the members of the family. They are interested in what their children are thinking and feeling, and they are not threatened by their children holding different thoughts than their own. At the same time, parents of securely attached children are very ready to share their own thoughts, feelings, dreams, and values with their children. When these parents demonstrate a habitual openness and interest in their children's minds, their children are equally interested in knowing their own minds and their parents' minds.

Though we are speaking of the child's emotional regulation and reflective skills separately for the purpose of describing them, in practice they are interwoven, which is the case for the securely attached child. Her emotional regulation skills enable her to better reflect and create stories about the events of her life, and her ability to make sense of things makes it easier to regulate the emotions associated with these events. It is the interwoven nature of these affective and reflective skills that enables coherent stories of stressful events to develop. For example, in DDP, the conversations that are the most therapeutic are known as affective-reflective dialogues because of their joint active presence in generating both the safety and exploration needed to cocreate new stories.

These reflective abilities are organized into internal working models, which are affective-cognitive schema for our sense of self and of other. For securely attached children, these schema involve responsiveness, warmth, and trust; whereas for insecurely attached children, they involve anger, mistrust, indifference, and anxiety or fears. For the disorganized attached child in particular, the schema, as it is directed toward self, is likely to be embedded in shame, which will restrict the child's readiness to reflect on himself. When asked about his thoughts, feelings, and motives, the disorganized attached child often responds with "I don't know!" And they are very often being truthful! They have spent many years avoiding looking inside. If they were to look within, they would most likely only find chaotic, poorly integrated, partially formed experiences of events that were devaluing. The insecure child is highly likely to conceal his vulnerable experiences of self and other behind rigid defenses of anger and indifference. It is the responsibility of the securely attached (known as autonomous attachment) adult to be able to perceive the vulnerability that lies beneath these defenses. The adult needs to see the qualities of the child that were evident before the child developed the insecure—and especially disorganized—attachment patterns.

In the above example both Michael and his parents, Sarah and Jon, were likely to misperceive each other's intentions, create negative assumptions about each other's motives, react to each other with defensiveness, and either attack or withdraw from the relationship. As this became an ongoing pattern in their lives, they all were more likely to experience pervasive shame, which further undermined their ability to be hopeful and to engage in relationship repair. For therapy to be of value, it needed to first create safety for Sarah and Tom—when seen alone—and then to create safety for the three of them, so that they could reflect on the stressful and shameful events of their relationship while remaining emotionally regulated. This may open the road to engaging in more behaviorally focused treatments when indicated, such as cognitive behavioral therapy, which could help Michael manage some of his attributions. But this is more possible, we believe, after safety, relationships, regulation, and reflection have been addressed. This, in essence, is the approach of this book.

ONGOING RELATIONSHIP REPAIR

As a parent is getting to know her child, interacting with her infant in reciprocal, nonverbal communications, she often is out-of-sync with her child's expressions. As she continuously monitors the presence of reciprocity, she frequently fine-tunes the interaction to achieve synchrony. This is known as interactive repair, and it is characteristic of the interactions of parents and infants who are both securely attached.

The need for ongoing relationship repair is necessary for any and all attachment relationships that are to maintain features of attachment security. All close relationships involve times of separations, misattunements, conflicts, misunderstandings, and competing responsibilities that need to be seen, acknowledged, and repaired in order to maintain trust in the relationship. Without ongoing repair, relationships either become stagnant from avoiding deeper meanings or they become highly conflictual, as they are unable to synchronize deeper meanings that exist between the two members of the dyad. Both situations place the relationship at risk of ending or of no longer serving its attachment-enhancing functions.

Relationship repair is often a challenge for individuals who are not securely attached. Relationship events are often perceived as having greater meaning than they are likely to have, stemming from their lack of confidence in the strength of the relationship. These individuals choose to solve relationship issues by making a superficial agreement, by being compliant, or by overlooking challenges to the relationship. Without repair, the conflicts and misperceptions are likely to become greater, and if the problem in the relationship is eventually discussed again, it is often done so with a degree of anger and shame that makes any resolution and repair extremely unlikely to occur.

In DDP, when the conversation leads to defensiveness and the need for relationship repair, the therapist sees this as an opportunity to deepen the relationship through successful repair. Both parent and child are discovering that a conflict can be explored safety when the parents are committed to understanding their child's experience without judgment. By committing to continuously repairing the relationship, the parents are communicating that the relationship is more important than the conflict. When the child senses that his experiences, which led to his behavior, are understood and addressed without judgment, he is much less likely to be defensive about his behavior. This often creates vulnerability in the child, and when the parents feel safe, they comfort their distressed child. After that, the "behavioral problems" tend to dissipate and they becomes more open to parental guidance.

It is not surprising that Michael and his parents found relationship repair to be very difficult. Whenever they attempted to address a problem, it was addressed with defensiveness and a lack of effort to understand each other. When they avoided a problem, it would return at a later date, even larger than it had been originally. Using attachment perspective processes, the problems were addressed in the context of the attachment relationship, without defensiveness and shame. Sarah and Jon were able to experience empathy for Michael's vulnerability that led to his challenging behaviors. These behaviors were now seen as alerts to challenges in their relationship rather than as an inherent characteristic of Michael.

SUMMARY

Attachment theory and principles have an important place in mental health interventions for children and their families. DDP utilizes attachment principles in therapy to facilitate features of attachment security within the daily functioning of the child and family. Specific goals involve developing trust within reciprocal engagements and developing the emotional and reflective skills needed to facilitate healthy attachment-based relationships. Just as attachment security in young children is facilitated by synchronized affective conversations between the child and her parents, so too are such affective conversations central to the attachment perspective in therapy. These conversations incorporate affective and reflective components and are characterized by continuous nonverbal communications that convey transforming intersubjective experiences. These conversations are also brought into synchrony with the child and her parent through ongoing interactive repair. Over the course of this therapeutic process, the child gradually develops a coherent autobiographical narrative. This narrative includes skills of relating, regulating, and reflecting that will likely enhance her development and mental health.

In the next chapter, we will explore the extensive research foundations of attachment theory. This body of research helps us to understand the attachment-based developmental pathways leading to both mental health and resiliency as well as to a variety of disorders. This will be followed, in the remaining chapters, by elaborate descriptions of the various aspects of DDP, as they address the attachment-related challenges of the child and parents who are receiving therapy.

chapter two

Attachment, Development, and Mental Health

———————————

The subject of this book, attachment and mental health, requires us to ask what at first seems a fairly simple question: "What is the relationship between attachment and mental health?" Over thirty years of research in the field of developmental psychopathology shows us that there are no straightforward and simple answers. Instead the answer lies, as it does in many disciplines, in a more complex interplay of factors, in this case with attachment as the frame to a picture of how the impact of life's stresses and strains may either increase the risk of disorder or push against one's resilience due to certain developmentally acquired or intrinsic (e.g., genetic) characteristics. As attachment theory would predict, the research also demonstrates that attachment influences developmental outcomes that are either commonly found in or associated with disorder. So, if we are to find an answer to our initial question, we need to ask a broader, richer one: "How is attachment related to development *and* mental health?"

As clinicians, we share a common interest in mechanisms that may explain how the difficulties of the family before us have come to pass and what maintains them. We need an entry point for our interventions. In this chapter, we begin by reviewing what is known about the broad associations between attachment and general patterns of disorder, namely externalizing (behavioral) and internalizing (emotional) disorders. To understand what we find, we need to return to the value of attachment theory as a developmental model. In so doing, we revisit important developmental concepts in the research that will be helpful to our practices as well as to our understanding of the literature. In Chapter 1, we described how attachment theory predicts the emergence of two important areas of development: 1) emotional regulation and 2) our internal working models for relationships between ourselves and the world around us that typify trust and a sense of safety with ourselves and others (referred to as social cognition in some research). Our intention now is to take these predictions into the realm of the research evidence. We review these as two potential mechanisms to see how they are associated with attachment and also with mental health. A detailed review of the literature is beyond the scope of this chapter; we found the reviews by DeKlyen and Greenberg (2016) and Thompson (2016) very helpful, and the interested reader is directed there.

When you picked up this book, you may have asked yourself "Why might my attention to the attachment relationship help my work with children with mental health problems?" We hope to begin to answer this question from a theoretical and research base in this chapter. Subsequent chapters move into the ways in which attention to the attachment relationship can help. For now, our brief response to this important question is: Based on the research evidence, we propose that DDP is a developmentally sound approach grounded in attachment theory. DDP seeks to address some of the common mechanisms related to both attachment and mental health difficulties. We consider the role of genetic aspects or other biological factors to the development of mental illness, but our focus here is on the role of attachment in mental health. Let us now begin our journey into the attachment research so we can provide you with a fuller and more satisfying answer by the end of this chapter.

ASSOCIATIONS BETWEEN ATTACHMENT AND MENTAL HEALTH DISORDERS

The finding that some 40% of the general population might have an insecure pattern challenged some early notions that research of this kind would find straightforward associations with psychiatric disorder because disorders never tend to approach such rates (Green & Goldwyn, 2002). The identification of the disorganized attachment category (Main & Solomon, 1990) has probably yielded more fruitful associations in this area (Green & Goldwyn, 2002), with research examining only the three original categories showing generally weaker associations (DeKlyen & Greenberg, 2016). Disorganized insecurity tends to be associated more with high risk samples who may have had early experiences of maltreatment or adversity (90%; Cicchetti, Rogosch, and Toth, 2006) compared to lower risk samples (15%; Van IJzendoorn, Schuengel, & Bakermans-Kranenburg, 1999). A review of the studies has consistently indicated some association, with conclusions clustering around insecurity of attachment but particularly disorganized insecurity as a generic, predisposing risk factor to mental health difficulties in children and adolescents. Taking a broad view, we now consider whether there are differences between the main categories of disorder, such as the internalizing versus externalizing disorders commonly seen in child and family work, and their links with attachment security. Meta-analyses are useful here to gain some consensus. Therefore, we turn our attention to two recent and contemporaneous meta-analyses to get an oversight for this broad discussion. We first consider externalizing difficulties and their links with attachment.

When we consider the associations between externalizing problems (such as disorders of conduct) and attachment security, there seems to be better evidence for a stronger relationship with attachment than for internalizing difficulties, such as anxiety and depression. For disorders of conduct, a comprehensive meta-analysis by Fearon, Bakermans-Kranenburg, Van IJzendoorn, Lapsley, and Roisman (2010) reviewed studies comprising nearly 6000 children. They found many differences in the methods and findings of these studies. Their results showed that, overall, disorganized attachment was a risk factor for later externalizing problems and this effect was generally much greater than for avoidant and ambivalent attachment, though avoidant insecurity had at least some association with later externalizing problems. However, the best, albeit modest, prediction came when gender (being male) was added: the results suggest that girls with disorganized attachment are at relatively lower risk of developing a disorder of this kind.

For disorders of an internalizing nature, such as anxiety and depression, meta-analysis again found that there were many studies with differing conclusions. Different methods of measurement accounted for the variation in results; questionnaires predicted relationships more strongly than direct measures of attachment. Also, many of the studies that showed some links examined only three classifications of attachment. Some studies found no associations at all. In their meta-analysis, Brumariu & Kerns (2010) sought to control for the number of classifications used. They found that, overall, there were only modest associations between attachment insecurity and anxiety and depression. This relationship tended to be stronger in adolescence than childhood. For those studies that looked only at three categories, ambivalence emerged as a predictor of anxiety, but not for depression, in preadolescence. When all four classifications were considered, disorganized attachment style better predicted internalizing difficulties, overall and also specifically for depression, than ambivalent attachment.

So, if the strength of the relationship between attachment insecurity and the common patterns of disorder that we would recognize in many clinics is modest, what can we conclude from this research? We might think of insecurity, particularly disorganized insecurity, as being a general risk factor to developing disorder. In the other direction, security of attachment might be seen as a protective factor. But this research does not fully inform the clinician of the ways in which some of these connections may arise. Our answer lies in the field of developmental psychopathology. By emphasizing the developmental outcomes associated with attachment, this research helps us locate the mechanisms that lead to and maintain disorders. If we are to apply this research to the families before us, we need to return to attachment theory and its roots as a developmental model in explaining normative and abnormal development.

GETTING BACK ON THE RIGHT TRACK

> From its inception, attachment theory was a theory of psychopathology as well as a theory of normal development.
> — Sroufe, Carlson, Kevy, & Egeland, 1999, p. 1

Put this way, attachment theory would seem to be well positioned to help study the development of mental disorder and pathology. John Bowlby (see Sroufe, 2013) used a simple yet useful analogy, that of a railway track, to explain the path to health or disorder. This analogy brings us to some important principles of developmental psychopathology. Some of these have also been highlighted and explained by DeKlyen & Greenberg (2016) in reviewing the research in this area and some of these theoretical principles are also covered here. Understanding these helps to convey the realities, richness and subtlety we are likely to see in our clinical work and tease out the more complex relationship between attachment and mental health. Taking a branch line away from the mainline of normal development and well-being could, under certain conditions, mean potential disorder. The opportunity to return to the main line would decrease the further the individual traveled down the "wrong track" (Sroufe, 2013). Equally, traveling one branch line away from the mainline of normal development does not mean pathology is inevitable. It may be helpful in some cases to see this more as a maladaptation, a key concept in attachment theory (Green & Goldwyn, 2002). In attachment terms, these maladaptations happen if the pattern of insecurity shows itself to lead to changes that, when faced with stress, make a disorder more possible (including gene x environment interactions). This also means that positive changes in life circumstances may not be made. For example, a child who has developed profound mistrust of adults (which served them well to keep them safe), due to their history of abuse, may then struggle to adapt to a safe and trustworthy adoptive family. It is helpful for us to think about how insecure patterns may have worked for our clients before even though they may no longer serve them well. As a developmental model, attachment theory does not pathologize but instead emphasizes the course of patterns of relationships over time may be seen as adaptive or maladaptive depending on the relational circumstances. It gives us a broader and more compassionate view of the path our clients have taken: "There but for the grace of God go I."

The route of travel down this railway of life and development is also influenced by understanding that there may be more than one way to reach a destination or that one way may take us in many directions. Although a young person may be suffering from a certain mental health problems, their origins may differ from other children. Attachment may have a role, but it also may not. It is important to hold this in mind when considering why we may not find an inevitable path for all children between one risk or protective factor and a given disorder. Even in the face of the same adversity, some children may struggle, and others may not. These are the principles of equifinality and multifinality. In other words, many factors may lead to the same outcome (equifinality) or the same factor may lead to many outcomes (multifinality). Going further into the potential mechanisms of these pathways, the differential susceptibility hypothesis (Ellis, Boyce, Belsky, Bakermans-Kranenburg, & Van IJzendoorn, 2011) is a more recent addition to developmental psychopathology which helps us understand the real life variance we may see between children and their outcomes in life. This hypothesis helps us understand that people are likely to have a different neurobiological susceptibility to their environments. For example, this hypothesis predicts that those children who seem vulnerable to adversity, and potentially the worse for it, may also be "susceptible" to responding just as much, but in the positive direction, when their environment changes for the better. Similarly, those who appear unaffected during times of difficulty may prove to be equally unresponsive to positive environments. This susceptibility to a new environmental condition may also extend to the provision of therapy. While this is not to say apparently susceptible children will necessarily do well in therapy, it is likely that different children will respond differently, depending on their past responses to positive and negative experiences in life. Ellis and colleagues (2011) proposed that this may explain why some interventions do not find large effects because it is cancelled out by such individual differences because studies are unlikely to select children with certain susceptibility profiles (Ellis et al., 2011).

It is important that we practitioners know when positive change is possible and maybe also by how much. Developmental systems theory also offers us some assistance. This theory proposes that the chances for positive change will depend on how far down the branch line toward potential disorder the child has traveled or, in other words, how far from normal development the child is at any given point (Sroufe, 2013). Attachment theory predicts that though internal working models may be formed early in life, this does not mean they are fixed for all relationships. They can change. For example, a study of adolescents in foster care showed that attaining a secure attachment with a foster caregiver is not only linked with fewer behavior difficulties, but can also be present when the child may also have insecure representations of the relationship with their birth parents (Joseph, O'Connor, Briskman, Maughan, & Scott, 2014).

Finally, attachment theory is also a very useful model to understand that there is a circular process whereby the child brings to the environment his own influence, shaping what resources can be made available to them, just as the environment may shape the child. As Sroufe et al. (1999) neatly put it: "Child and context are mutually transforming" (p. 2). As development progresses, there may be continuities and discontinuities in development, with some of these changes becoming more self-organizing and internalized. These characteristics of the child then influence their interaction with the world as they meet it. For example, the well-regulated and positively disposed child may elicit kinder, more helpful responses from a teacher than a dysregulated and hostile child. Even small children with insecure patterns may close down the nurturing from their foster caregivers (Stovall & Dozier, 2000). This may be where much of the work for foster and adoptive parents seems to lie, in helping build new working models of relationships. We will return to this process in more detail as it applies to parents in Chapter 4 and to schools and communities in Chapter 8.

In summary, attachment theory can, in principle, help us understand the different pathways children may have toward health and development or toward a greater chance of pathology or disorder. As a developmental model, attachment theory helps us understand and identify some of the reasons why children have different outcomes and different stories that have led them to a given point in their lives. If we remember these principles of development, our understanding of our clients is enriched. Often the mental health setting may emphasize only the pathology; that is, this approach might prioritize the question "What is the problem?" Of course this is important. But there may be less of an emphasis on developmental mechanisms and adaptations that have now gone awry; this latter approach would ask "How did we get here?" We have seen that attachment insecurity may indicate the possibility that there was a worse start in the child's journey through development; that the branch line is beginning to move away from health and development. However, if we are to understand the mechanisms involved in a way that has clinical value to the families in our clinics, we need to look more closely at how attachment relates to development that may either jeopardize or support health. We are now going to review some of the evidence for two cornerstones of attachment theory, emotional regulation and social cognition (related to internal working models), as two key mechanisms of the four, which are associated with both attachment and disorder, proposed by DeKlyen & Greenberg (2016).

EMOTIONAL REGULATION

As discussed in Chapter 1, a fundamental function of attachment relationships is the extent to which the emotional states of the infant, child, or adult are regulated by the attachment figure (Mikulincer & Shaver, 2012). This is done in many ways, using touch, gestures, facial expressions, and tone of voice, and is a truly reciprocal process with the infant and parent both playing their part (Field, 1994). The absence or presence of regulating parental behavior has a potentially big effect on the organization of the infant's capacity, at a neurobiological level, to regulate their distress as they develop and age. Dysregulating mental states in the parent (usually frightening or frightened; Main & Solomon, 1990), which is most associated with the disorganized category of attachment, might typify the biggest risks to the development of emotional regulation in the child.

Over time, the capacity to regulate emotional distress becomes more internalized as the child moves outside of the parent–child relationship (Calkins, 2004). As Dozier and colleagues (2006) describe, the capacity for regulation is "at first dyadic, with the parent taking an important coregulating role in scaffolding regulation. With effective smooth dyadic regulation, the infant can gradually come to take over regulatory functions independently" (p. 768). As they age, this would place children and young people with emotional regulation problems and without the presence of a regulating caregiver at a potential developmental disadvantage. In this way, emotional regulation difficulties are seen as risk factors or important mechanisms in many disorders, including externalizing disorders, such as oppositional defiant disorder (Cavanagh, Quinn, Duncan, Graham, & Balbuena, 2017) and behavioral problems (Halligan et al., 2013), and internalizing disorders, such as depression (Silk, Shaw, Forbes, Lane, & Kovacs, 2006) and anxiety disorders (Suveg & Zeman, 2004). In the other direction, the capacity to control emotion and impulses, for example, have been associated with secure attachment, less alcohol abuse, academic achievement, and better interpersonal relationships later in life (Tangney, Baumeister, & Boone, 2004; Aldao, Nolen-Hoeksema, & Schweizer, 2010). Using coregulation to regulate the emotional states of the child who lacks these capacities is an important focus in several attachment-informed approaches to addressing attachment and also, potentially, to addressing adverse outcomes.

The theoretical role of attachment on emotional regulation is consistent with the concept of the stress buffering role of the parent to child relationship. This concept is where interest has deepened to measure physiological markers of stress such as cortisol in children. Cortisol is a stress hormone whose presence in high levels indicates that the stress response system is being activated. Cortisol is also present during the day, even in the absence of perceived stress: it normally rises in the morning and tails off toward the evening, permitting us to sleep. Research shows that in at-risk groups, such as foster children who have experienced both disruptive attachment experiences and early adversity, have altered cortisol production across the day (Bernard, Butzin-Dozier, Rittenhouse, & Dozier, 2010). This alteration may be a reversal of the normal pattern of cortisol across the day or a flattened profile of either consistently high or consistently low production. Interestingly, consistently low cortisol production is linked with conduct disorder in older children (Fairchild et al., 2008). Even under the most stressful situations, such as maltreatment, the presence of secure relationship patterns can have a protective role. For example, Alink, Cicchetti, Kim, and Rogosch (2009) found that in a sample of maltreated children, those who had a secure pattern of relatedness with their parent, did not experience the same emotional regulation problems and therefore were less likely to have externalizing or internalizing difficulties. In this way, the caregiver who can confer this stress buffering effect on their child, by fostering emotional regulation, can protect them from poor outcomes even when they have had disruptive histories.

Mary Dozier's pioneering work with fostered toddlers is an excellent example of how actively attending to the attachment relationship with insecure children can help emotional regulation develop. This research has shown that even a short program involving following the child's lead, increasing touch, and providing nurturing even when the infants may not signal a need for regulation and proximity can lead to profound changes in cortisol production, returning them to near-typical daytime patterns (Dozier et al., 2006). Such positive physiological changes from this intervention can persist for many years. Nine-year-old children who participated in an intervention program like the one outlined above in their early years, showed positive differences in vagal tone, measured by taking respiratory sinus arrhythmia measurements (the heart rate increases with the intake of breath, showing that more rapid breathing reflects poorer regulation; Tabachnick, Raby, Goldstein, Zajac, & Dozier, 2019).

Emotional regulation is also a feature of the executive functions. Executive functions are the cognitive capacities for self-monitoring, utilizing working memory, managing impulses, making flexible shifts in thinking, and affective capacity for emotional (self) regulation (Stuss, 2011). These abilities are associated with the prefrontal cortex, a brain region associated with extensive postnatal growth that is both experience expectant and experience dependent. As a measure of the quality of early experience, attachment theory can assist our understanding of the development of children's neurodevelopmental systems in particular (Low & Webster, 2016). While executive function deficits are implicated in several disorders commonly found in child mental health clinics, such as attention deficit hyperactivity disorder (Willcutt, Doyle, Nigg, Faraone, & Pennington, 2005), autism (Pennington & Ozonoff, 1996), and antisocial behavior (Morgan & Lilienfeld, 2000). Attachment has been associated with both executive functioning and disorder. Low and Webster (2016) found that disorganized insecurity (but not security or other forms of insecurity) predicted poor planning ability and other executive functions. This deficit explained the presence of behavioral problems in children with disorganized insecurity. This suggests there may be a specific concern about children with disorganized insecurity and later outcomes; though they did also find that other forms of insecurity predicted behavior problems but without the link to diminished executive functions. Indeed, neuroimaging studies also demonstrate that capacities for emotional regulation, mediated in the prefrontal cortex and related structures in the amygdala, are disrupted by maltreatment (Callaghan & Tottenham, 2016), which itself confers risk of the development of disorganized security. Bernier, Beauchamp, Carlson, and Lalonde (2015) found that secure attachment in infancy predicted better executive functioning in children several years later, when they were beginning school. One potential explanation for this finding, suggested by Bernier and colleagues, is that the more secure infants had mothers who had better executive function who could then regulate and scaffold their children better. Maternal caregiving and executive functions are associated, and though one can imagine that well-regulated executive functioning in parents could relate to attachment security, no study has directly examined this. Waters and colleagues (2010) carefully investigated the processes that might be involved in the development of emotional regulation and attachment in a study of mothers and their four-and-a-half-year-olds under conditions of mild stress. The researchers were interested in whether mothers and children reported the same emotional experience after a mildly emotionally dysregulating task for the child. The study assumed that being able to recognize the emotional state of the child is important in emotional regulation. While the parent and child participated in this mildly frustrating task they were videotaped. After this, the parent and child were interviewed about the video tape of them performing the task which was then evaluated and rated by trained observers. Waters and colleagues found that in secure relationships, these mothers matched the emotions felt and expressed by their children better than mothers in insecure relationships. But they also found that conversations about negative emotions were tolerated in the interview when the mother accepted the child's emotions and there was a secure attachment relationship. This acceptance of all emotional states, combined with a secure relationship and a degree of emotional literacy for negative emotions, places children in a better position to be regulated and to interact with the world in a way that serves them well. It is also, as we shall explore, linked with our next developmental outcome topic: social cognition.

Overall, this research suggests that attachment helps set the foundation for the growth in emotional regulation. This opens potential pathways for moving further away from disorders of various types. Secure children with better emotional regulation and executive function may, under stressful conditions, be in a better position to negotiate these events and stay on the right track. We have also learned that actively addressing the insecure relationship and encouraging acceptance of negative experiences in the child can foster emotional regulation. We will learn in the next section that, protected with this vital developmental armor, these children may also be able to signal and enlist people to assist them, using their internal working models of relationships and benefiting from coregulation through subsequent secure and sensitive responding. How trusting they are to signal the need for others is the next stage in our journey through the research literature.

SOCIAL COGNITION

An interest in the capacity for social interaction with others is a natural counterpart to the development of attachment. It is important in understanding how children may develop into socially flexible and capable adults with better psychological well-being. Indeed, the research in this area has found links with attachment security and a range of potentially positive developmental outcomes that can be classed as reflecting social cognition, which includes emotional understanding, social competence, emotional competence, attributional style, and social problem-solving (i.e., how attachment may influence how children trust or not their parents for socially relevant information; see Thompson, 2016 for a more detailed review). As we will discuss, these attributes may explain why securely attached children are more likely to be successful with their peers. The internal working models, as templates for the self and other in relationships, are of relevance here. As we mentioned in Chapter 1, Bowlby's proposal was that these emotionally driven mental representations of the self and others typified patterns of social interaction. These begin with the parent, and then generalizes to the world. In secure relationships, this enables them to not only understanding their own emotions but also the emotions of others. Being able to function reflectively means they do well in social relationships. If they have positive views of the self and others, they are therefore positively predisposed toward people, and we might define this as being trusting. There is a sense of safety *first* for these individuals.

For the purposes of this chapter, we focus on Internal Working Models (IWMs) as they are potentially reflected in the social realm of relationships; that is the attributions of the social world and the understanding of the perspectives of others and the self (reflective functioning) described broadly in this section and the literature as social cognition.

Attachment theory would predict that secure children are likely to engage well with the social world, seeing themselves and others benignly, and they are also more able to understand the views of others, their thoughts and intentions. They trust more instinctively. They are comfortable and feel safe in their own skins. They are able to be reflective about their own mental states and those of others. The avoidant child is likely to disregard and dismiss the need for others, being closed to the minds of others and may be prone to isolation because they are mistrustful. The ambivalent child seeks proximity while lacking the capacity for self-regulation and viewing themselves as ineffective. They overvalue others and mistrust their own resilience. The disorganized child may develop a negative and hostile view of themselves and the world, potentially inducing reciprocal patterns with others who react defensively to them, inadvertently perpetuating their profound mistrust of people. These children mistrust both themselves and others. So, what does some of the research tell us about whether these social cognitive styles are linked to attachment styles?

Particularly interesting in light of our focus on emotional regulation, Denham, Blair, Schmidt, and DeMulder (2002) examined the attachment, emotional regulation, and emotional understanding of three-year-old children and then assessed their social competence (as rated by teachers and peers) two years later, at age five. At follow up, children with a history of insecure attachment were more likely to demonstrate emotional incompetence, typified by a lack of regulated anger and poorer emotional understanding. Children with this kind of emotional incompetence were associated with negative peer ratings and teacher reports indicating the children were oppositional and more difficult than their peers. The authors also point to the importance of attachment in the development of emotional regulation *and* emotional understanding. They emphasize that secure attachment may have an early protective role in avoiding pathways to behavioral difficulties and disorders. For example, insecure attachment and a negative and mistrustful interpretation of the world might explain the early routes of negative attributional biases about peers that are found in older children with chronic aggression (Burks, Laird, Dodge, Pettit, & Bates, 1999). Indeed, Zajac, Bookhout, Hubbard, Carlson, and Dozier (2018) found that disorganized attachment (but not security or other forms of insecurity) in infancy predicted similar hostile biases and aggressive intentions when the children were eight years old compared to children who were rated as securely attached to their mothers. The role of internal working models as templates for relationships seems to be supported by these findings.

There is some evidence that secure working models of relationships are more positive in patterns of attribution about others. Secure children in preschool make more friendly attributions to characters in a story-based task than do their insecure counterparts (Cassidy, Kirsh, Scolton, & Parke, 1996). These and other studies suggest secure children have developed a positive disposition to engage with the world. However, the continuing role of security in the child's life has an important role to play in social relationships. Measuring attachment across time points (12, 24, and 36 months) indicated that the link between security and better social information processing was stronger when they were secure across more than one assessment (Raikes & Thompson, 2008). Belsky and Fearon (2002) also found that continued sensitive parenting along with secure attachment in infancy predicted better social capabilities. These studies suggest that having continued sensitivity and security, from an initial secure classification, leads to better social functioning, which is in contrast to insecure children and especially those with externalizing problems.

There is also some evidence that attachment classification accounts for the degree of trust in the judgments of others. As part of a longitudinal study (Corriveau, Harris, Meins, Fernyhough, Arnott et al., 2009), 147 children aged about five years were presented with two tasks. In the first they witnessed their mother and a stranger giving a different name for a certain hybrid animal which could either support the mother or stranger's claims of what it could be called (e.g., exactly two half animals combined as an image). In the second task, the hybrid animal was more clearly a certain animal, but in this task, the stranger's claim was better supported by the image (e.g., more one animal than the other). Overall, they found that children tended to prefer their mother's claims over the strangers in the first task and when the mother was evidently "wrong" in the second task they agreed with the stranger. However, when attachment classification was examined, they found some interesting differences. The study found that secure children tended to rely on the mother when she was truthful (first task) but could go their own way when she was intentionally being untruthful (second task). They could trust others but also themselves; demonstrating a degree of flexibility which contrasted with the other forms of insecurity. Avoidant children tended to dismiss their mother's claims even when she might be truthful (e.g., in the first task). They went their own way, which is consistent with the prediction we would make regarding the patterns of internal working models in this group who may be more self-reliant and closed off from others. In contrast, ambivalent children tended to rely on their mother regardless of her accuracy. This pattern is also consistent with the expected internal working models, which highlight high dependency on others and low confidence in their own capacities. As might be predicted, disorganized children were not systematic at all and displayed a pattern consistent with neither trusting themselves or others in an organized way. This research supports how attachment may influence trust in others but also can show resilience and flexibility in interpreting the social world.

Even making a simple connection with a child can make a difference to their openness to someone else's ideas. This demonstrates how important relationship can be for the acceptance of social information. In a simple yet elegant study, eighteen-month-old children were presented with two ambiguous yet attractive toy-like objects and an experimenter who would express a preference for one of the objects by either smiling or making a facial expression of disgust. The infants followed the experimenter's preference only if the experimenter had directly engaged the child (e.g., saying the child's name) before the task began (Egyed, Király, & Gergely, 2013).

How this "social" information is transmitted corresponds with the potential role of mentalization, another word for "reflective functioning" (Fonagy & Target, 1997). Fonagy, Gergely, and Target (2007) state: "Mentalising refers both to reflecting on the contents of others' mindsand to having knowledge of one's own intentions, desires and thoughts" (p. 297). This is in keeping with findings relating to emotional competence in children and how they make social decisions about others. From work initially on theory of mind (which focuses on the ability to take a perspective of others, mentalization, or reflective functioning, goes further to having a theory of one's own *and* another's mind. Research has shown how this capacity in the parent is linked with secure attachment in their infant (Fonagy, Steele,

Steele, Moran, & Higgitt, 1991) and is characterized by how well they maintain a stance of not knowing and being open to uncertainty about the minds of others but also their own mental states. What is so compelling in this particular study is that researchers measured this capacity in the parent before the child was born. Furthermore, when the children in this cohort, born to these parents, were followed up at five years of age (Fonagy, Steele, Steele, & Holder, 1997), the securely attached children performed better on social cognitive tasks (as cited in Luyten, Nijssens, Fonagy, & Mayes, 2017) than insecure children. In this way, the proposal here might be that attachment in the parent, characterized by reflective functioning, influences the quality of the attachment relationship and consequently the child's social cognitive capacities. The search to explain how attachment status in the parent may predict the attachment classification of the child to their parent has been explored before and with no mechanism yet identified this has been referred to as the "transmission gap" (Van IJzendoorn, 1995). But further insights can be gleaned from the concept of reflective functioning for working with families and helping understand links with mental health difficulties. The role of attachment through the presence of reflective functioning is proposed as being important to another important function of the attachment relationship; the transmission of "epistemic trust."

Epistemic trust is defined as the "trust in the authenticity and personal relevance of interpersonally transmitted knowledge about how the social environment works and how best to navigate it" (Fonagy, Campbell, & Bateman, 2017, p. 177). Children who are able to use knowledge through a secure relationship (which offers reflective functioning by way of sensitivity and attunement from the parent) are likely to adapt quickly to the important knowledge around them with the necessity for practice or self-discovery (which may be risky). Where reflective function is depleted, as in an insecure relationship, the child is developmentally disadvantaged, and their mental health is at greater risk. This means that attachment has an important role in social communication of the social context the child finds themselves in. Fonagy and colleagues (2017) propose that this is a hitherto underestimated function of the attachment relationship and probably so important that the role of epistemic mistrust has also been proposed as a common factor in predicting psychopathology (Fonagy et al., 2017). Epistemic trust may have an important role in understanding and measuring how children see the world in the way Bowlby's IWMs would predict Fonagy et al., 2017). In the clinic, engaging this understanding would help us see whether or not a child may rely on others and it may also go further in explaining the child's relationship with the community and its institutions. For example, a child with epistemic mistrust, due to abuse and the absence of reflective functioning in their attachment relationship, may close their connection with their community, regarding teachers, members of the public, and also view us with suspicion and hostility. Indeed, there is evidence that parent–child security also predicts a child's security with teachers and others (Williford, Carter, & Pianta, 2016). Understanding this would not only be of great value, but a route to embrace this understanding with our clients would seem essential if our ideas and interventions are to be accepted by our clients when they show insecurity. The concept of epistemic trust has been central to the development of successful work with hard to reach youth in the UK, using the AMBIT model (Adaptive Mentalization-Based Integrative Treatment) which actively engages mentalization/reflective functioning to facilitate a connection with the child's epistemic position (Bevington, Fuggle, Fonagy, Target, & Asen, 2013).

Taken together, this body of research supports a range of helpful social cognitive capacities associated with secure attachment for a pathway of greater resilience and well-being. There are also links between emotional regulation and these capacities for social cognition, including reflective functioning as a vital developmental outcome of secure attachment; one cannot be without the other, it seems. The role of attachment in shaping the individual's view of the world does seem to follow John Bowlby's internal working models. The research we have reviewed in this section points us to critical features (which are embedded in the DDP model), such as the relevance of continually providing sensitive care and of actively engaging and accepting the child's story of themselves and others, that are essential for children to move toward healthier and more resilient branch lines of development and away from their present mental health difficulties.

CONCLUSIONS

We began this chapter by asking if we might understand how attachment may explain mental health problems. The research shows us that the more meaningful and robust answer comes when we see how attachment influences development rather than linking attachment directly with disorder (see Figure 2.1). As predicted by attachment theory, better emotionally regulated children, with a tendency to trust in themselves and others, are more likely to follow a path, notwithstanding other genetic factors that risk their well-being, of healthy development and resilience. Evidence has shown that attachment has a powerful influence changing physiology and neurobiological functioning. Secure children are more likely to be reflective about their minds and those of others, and they are more socially competent and capable of negotiating relationships as they grow. For the insecurely attached child, the path is more varied. These children may follow a disordered path if a pattern of mistrust and more limited emotional regulation becomes established and may eventually reach the threshold of disorder on that path. Children exposed to experiences that lead to them exhibit disorganized attachment are less able to manage their distress and emotional state. They may have hostile, mistrustful, and defensive responses to others, including potentially helpful relationships with teachers, people in the community and, yes, child mental health professionals. They may have long been on the route to disorder due to reciprocal patterns of negativity and hostility. For both patterns of security and patterns of insecurity, the child and environment are mutually transforming.

Before we link this evidence with practice, some words of caution are needed. We return to the developmental principles previously highlighted: Not all paths will lead to disorder. Change may be possible depending on how far down the line of a disorder pathway a child has followed. Not all children will respond to the same environment in the same way. Also, in some challenging environments, the presence of security is

Figure 2.1: Pathways Linking Attachment Security, Developmental Outcomes, and Mental Health

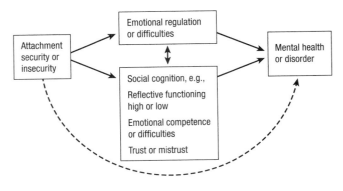

Dashed lines show modest links, firm lines show more robust links.

protective. Ongoing sensitivite parenting should not be taken for granted, even when security has been observed before. Furthermore, we are not proposing that we *know* that addressing these mechanisms is the way to treat disorder, as the links are not yet fully tested, though several interventions outside the attachment perspective have tackled some of mechanisms already (Kazdin, 1997). However, our view which is shared with others, is that these developmental mechanisms offer the clinician a point of entry since they are common in many disorders. Many disorders are characterized by regulation problems and/or social cognitive difficulties. This entry point identifies the angles for potential intervention alongside treatment for the specific symptoms of the particular disorder. Indeed, it has been argued that all psychotherapies seek to address emotional regulation (Cole, Michel, & Teti, 1994). The emphasis in this book, as it is in DDP, is that enhancing the developmental elements of emotional regulation and social cognition together, through active engagement in therapy and between the child and their care-givers in the way we describe in this book, may build resilience and address common factors that typify and also maintain disorder. This is but one path of recovery but it sets the foundation on which DDP is based as an attachment theory model of intervention.

Attending to the role of attachment security and the developmental outcomes it enhances has been emphasized by several authors and models. DDP as an attachment perspective shares the same emphasis. For example, Mikulincer and Shaver (2012) reviewed the evidence supporting an approaches which actively addressing the safety, emotional regulation, and elements of social cognition (e.g., IWMs) through the lens of attachment in adults with mental health problems:

> This evidence underscores the soothing, healing, therapeutic effects of actual support offered by relationship partners,

including therapists, and the comfort and safety offered by mental representations of supportive experiences and loving and caring attachment figures. The research evidence causes us to be optimistic about the utility of clinical interventions that increase clients' sense of attachment security. (p. 14)

Enhancing these same elements is seen as important for prevention and in treatment, contrasting this with other more disorder only driven approaches as described by Denham and colleagues (2002):

> Family-based prevention efforts, with parents aided in fostering secure attachments as well as emotional competence, are needed (Contreras et al., 2000; Denham, 1998). In contrast, Webster-Stratton's (1998) combination of parenting skills training and social skills training for children, although highly successful, does not include any focus on attachment and emotional competence. (p. 80)

Indeed, we have seen how attention to the regulatory and insecure aspects of a relationship can yield meaningful change in children, despite a history of maltreatment and adversity (Dozier et al., 2006). Joseph and colleagues (2014) report that this is also the case for adolescents who show behavioral difficulties with the same troubled backgrounds and that the site for changing their behavior may be through the attention to the attachment relationship: "Improving the quality of parent–child interactions in foster families may promote the formation of a secure attachment relationship and better psychological adjustment as a result" (p. 12).

Therefore, presented with a family in the clinic, the clinician who actively engages using patterns of emotional regulation and social cognition may be in a better position to offer the opportunity to acquire some of the developmental tasks we have presented here, which are often deficient in those with mental health difficulties. We have seen how acceptance of negative emotion may be relevant to emotional regulation between parent and child. Furthermore, understanding the child's lens for relationships, and potentially its origin, while actively engaging with the child and parent can facilitate the context for resolution and repair. This includes actively exploring their expectations of themselves and others including the therapist. Trust in the social information of the knowledge we share will depend on their internal working models of relationships. Thus, when meeting children with emotional regulation difficulties and insecure attachment, attending to their difficulties with emotional regulation and to their level of trust (reflected in their capacity to move toward the caregiver) is important in treating children presenting with difficulties or disorders of many kinds. Notwithstanding their specific mental health disorder, where there is insecurity of attachment—and especially disorganized insecurity—these children appear to have a cumulative, triple disadvantage: poorer emotional regulation capacities, less openness to interpersonal resolution, and fewer avenues for securing regulation and care. Take this working example:

> An eleven-year-old boy presents in clinic with persisting child-onset conduct problems. He shows the typical pattern of hostility to others with a tendency to misattribute their intentions as hostile. His emotions are unpredictable, changing quickly from one state to another. He seems more able to signal his distress through aggressive and angry interactions, with little or no signs of vulnerability. He is in trouble at school; his parents feel they have no influence on him; and he is out of the home more than he is in the home. Let us say we know his early history—which suggests that when

he was born his mother was depressed, unresolved about her own difficult upbringing, at times unpredictable, dysregulated when faced with his distress, and unavailable in varying measure—we can begin to see why he lacked the chances to develop the sense that others were available and regulating. His father's role presents a similar picture. Although he is present and employed, he too had a challenging childhood, including similar conduct problems and growing up with an alcoholic father. His father's "lessons in life" taught him to rely on himself and to minimize closeness with others. We can see how the internal working models of relationships (social cognition) of the eleven-year-old boy we are meeting now might have been adversely affected, skewed to keeping people at a distance and even being suspicious of their motivations. We could also predict that his opportunities for regulation of emotion were lacking in his formative early years, when he was dependent on others to develop these capacities, which has led to the current pattern that includes bouts of destructive and impulsive acts. If the problems with his parents persist in the present, this young man is unlikely to affiliate people with comfort and soothing; even when a motivated teacher who understands him attempts to help, their bids are rejected by the young man. In a similar way, he is a reluctant client. In short, considering his emotional regulation and internal models of relationships, it seems he is already a long way down the track toward a persistent disorder. If to this scenario we add that the family has low income, requiring both parents to work long, low-paid hours with few positive community opportunities, the picture worsens.

Where does the assessing clinician begin to use an attachment framework, such as DDP, to offer the chance for a better outcome? All that is relevant to begin this intervention is probably present in the room, specifically in how the young man and his parents relate to one another and to the clinician, albeit in the formality of a clinical setting. There are likely to be: hostile responses to bids of empathy and offers of help ("There is no point, don't try to change me."); invalidation of feelings ("He should sort himself out," says the father, distancing the boy from the chance of regulation); or overwhelming affect (the mother sits crying wordlessly when asked about her hopes for her son). Indeed, maintaining an approach that emphases the social cognition of the therapist or an active reflective stance can be challenged by such moments of emotional arousal (Fonagy & Luyten, 2009). In the chapters that follow, we outline how DDP seeks to develop the triad of 1) safety and trust, 2) emotional regulation, and 3) reflective functioning. We will return to and reference this triad frequently throughout the book.

As we have seen, there are close interrelationships between these three developmental domains, which are all touched by attachment. The next chapter describes the five components of DDP as an attachment-informed approach for addressing these developmental areas:

- PACE: Playfulness, Acceptance, Curiosity, Empathy
- Affective–Reflective Dialogue
- Follow-Lead-Follow
- Interactive Repair
- Speaking For and About

Throughout the rest of the book, we focus on key areas of development to illustrate how these five components may be used to enhance the resilience and development of these capacities for the benefit of children (and their parents) referred for mental health problems.

chapter three

Core Components of an Attachment-Based Therapy

Since creating safety for the child is the central function of attachment in development, safety must also be central in any model of therapy and care that is based on attachment principles. The therapist needs to be aware of how her presence and engagement will influence the child's and parents' sense of safety during every moment of every session. Whenever there is the slightest sign that the child or parent does not feel safe, the therapist needs to focus on re-establishing a sense of safety before going forward with any theme that is being explored. The central importance of safety will be evident in our discussion of all of the core components of DDP, the attachment-based model of therapy presented in this chapter.

As his therapist, you need to be aware of the child and his parents' needs for safety, and your moment-to-moment impact on their safety before you meet them each session in the waiting room. Before you meet them? Yes, because the child you are about to see will notice—really notice—everything that you do and say, and he will be utilizing his internal working models to decide whether he will be psychologically safe with you. The facial expressions that you make—out of the countless expressions that you might make—will create an initial impression as to how interested you are in him, the nature of your interest, and what your intentions are in being with him. Your voice prosody—rhythms, intensity, animation, variations—will convey whether you are accepting or evaluating the child—and it is important to remember that unconditional acceptance will create a greater sense of safety and readiness to engage than will the most positive evaluation.

You need always to be aware that the child you see may be defensive at times, and may also challenge you in an angry and defiant manner. And you need to not become defensive yourself, or he is not likely to feel safe enough to become open and engaged in the conversation that you will be trying to have with him. To inhibit your tendency to become defensive in response to his defiance, you will need to understand a bit of his history so that you can have compassion for the challenges that he has had to face. You will have to reflect on aspects of your own history with regard to whether or not any of your challenges might become activated. You will also need to be able to set aside any other stresses in your life outside of therapy (more about this and the importance of mindfulness in Chapter 8). If your mind wanders to other things, the child will very likely judge that you are not interested in him, that you are only seeing him because you are obligated to do so, or that you do not think that things will ever change.

Just as the child will be closely aware of your nonverbal expressions, you need to be aware of his expressions to better synchronize your social-emotional communications. The many years of research on infant–parent relationships conducted by Beatrice Beebe (2014), Colwyn Trevarthen (2001) and others have demonstrated how those face-to-face, moment-to-moment interactions between infant and parent are crucial for the development of both safety and attachment within the relationship as well as many other aspects of the infant's development. The infant notices every little thing you do and these ongoing non-verbal expressions are crucial for the developing relationship. Porges's polyvagal theory also shows us that our own sense of safety—how relaxed we are—will be conveyed in the subtle muscles of our face around our eyes, and the subtle expressions these muscles make are read by others and directly affect their physiological state. The same is true in therapy, no matter what approach is being offered. If the child is to feel safe and then use the relationship as a source of new social-emotional learning about the self and other, it will be these synchronized, nonverbal communications that both lead the way and maintain the ongoing safe-to-explore experiences that the child will need to benefit from the therapy. (We will say more about developing safety throughout the rest of this book.) With safety so established, the following five components of DDP can be therapeutic.

PACE: AN ATTACHMENT-BASED MANNER OF ENGAGEMENT

The therapist strives to have conversations with the child that enable the child to be open and engaged and will lead to developing the child's sense of safety and new learning. In DDP, the therapist has a general template for this process of relating with the child. A template that stresses reasoning, problem solving, and providing recommendations for change is not likely to create a sense of safety nor a readiness to explore new meanings—especially not at first. Of much greater value is for the therapist to maintain a relational attitude characterized by *playfulness*, *acceptance*, *curiosity*, and *empathy* (PACE).

When relating to their infant, a parent naturally notices the

expressions of the child, is thrilled about them, takes delight
in them, and actively wonders about their meanings. When
the child shows distress, the parent responds with comfort and
support. Any focus on the behavior itself is secondary. While
deeply engaged with the child, the parent's communications
are characterized by playfulness, acceptance, curiosity, and
empathy. These interactions involve the parent's sensitive and
responding presence, so the child develops trust in her and the
engagement becomes deeply reciprocal and meaningful to both
of them. Within this engagement, the parent is sensitive to her
child's affective expressions, noticing if the child needs her help
to stay regulated. She is also sensitive to her child's expressions
with regard to their possible meanings, and her empathic reading of her child facilitates the child's social cognitions. And
the parent is continually fine tuning these interactions, giving her child the experience of interactive repair. PACE helps
the child's caregiver—and therapist—to stay focused on their
relationship with the child, the child's affective experience, his
inner life, and the meanings inherent in what he is doing. In
therapy, it is the child—not the problem—that the therapist is
so interested in, discovering who this child is and finding ways
to enter into a conversation with him that maintains safety
while exploring all aspects of his life. While experiencing the
therapist's attitude of PACE, the child is likely to begin to settle
in, to let go of his defensive stance, and to begin to be open and
engaged with the therapist.

The four features of PACE are best expressed in a coherent,
complimentary manner, activating and integrating reflective
and affective states around both enjoyable or affirming themes
as well as stressful or shame inducing themes. As PACE becomes
the natural way of being with their child, parents are able to slow
down and not rush to make things better. Rather than focusing
on managing behavior before even knowing what the behav-

ior means, the parent—and therapist—prioritizes establishing a trusting connection with their child, and from the emerging reciprocal engagement, they are able to make sense of the worrisome behaviors. Only then is the adult able to have confidence in how to respond to the child.

The attitude of **PLAYFULNESS** is so often present in our engagements with young children. And for good reason! Playfulness conveys a sense of lightness and enjoyment that emerges simply by being in their presence. It demonstrates that relating with the child is important to us—and often fun for both of us! Being with her brings delight and pleasure. It creates a sense of closeness that is separate from affection. There is safety in this closeness. The relationship is being highlighted as the most important experience to us here and now, and any differences are secondary.

Playfulness also brings greater depth and breadth to the conversation that is developing between the therapist and child. Though the child still feels safe, when the therapist expresses herself playfully, there is likely to be some uncertainty in the child's experience that generates a greater focus on the therapist's nonverbal and verbal communications. This uncertainty creates some suspense—why is she saying that? Does she like me or not? Is she annoyed or is she gently teasing me? As the light teasing tone ends and the child realizes that the therapist was being playful, there is a sense that the therapist's words came from a place of liking the child, not being annoyed with her. This gentle teasing tends to generate a greater sense of safety for the child and to increase the child's desire to remain engaged in the conversation to see what happens next. When the conversation then flows into a stressful theme, often the child continues in the conversation, feeling safe and that the therapist truly likes her.

When we are smiling and laughing with our child, there is an experience of spontaneity and openness to whatever is happening. Joint laughter and enjoyment convey a sense of acceptance and ease, which are the opposites of shame and fear. Such shared joyful experiences are likely to create confidence that the conversation—and the relationship—are strong enough to handle any behavior or event that is being explored. One is not likely to convey such ease, even merriment, if the content about to be explored might end the relationship or uncover a situation that is hopeless.

Sometimes playful expressions withdraw into the background because the content is much too difficult or sad to experience as playful. But often, less stressful themes are made lighter and more approachable when the therapist finds a playful perspective to help the child hold onto the larger context, where the difficult theme does not seem so bad. Holding playfulness in mind, even when not being expressed, conveys a sense of hope and optimism that there are many positive reasons for finding joy and confidence in the days ahead. We will not be defeated by this stressful event, problem, or trauma! In doing this, the therapist is not minimizing the impact of the stressful event but rather helping the child to experience the larger, affirming context in which the event will become integrated and resolved.

EXAMPLE OF PLAYFULNESS:

CHILD: You know as much about my life as I know about life on the moon!

THERAPIST: So, you teach me, and I'll teach you! Did you know that the scientists are shocked to discover that the moon is really made out of cheese—Swiss cheese—which is why it has so many craters!

CHILD: You're crazier than I thought!

> **THERAPIST:** Not fair! Before you call me crazy, you have to first tell me something about yourself since I told you something about the moon!

It is always important to remember that what the therapist says to be playful may be experienced by the child as being sarcastic or as devaluing the child's experience. When that occurs, the therapist always repairs the relationship, avoiding any defensiveness.

The success of our engagement with the child and the conversations that develop rest on our **ACCEPTANCE** of the child and his experiences, not evaluations. Trusting that he is accepted, he is safe to explore himself, others, and the many events of his life. With acceptance, the child becomes open and engaged with the therapist, develops a sense of trust in their relationship, and is ready to influence and to be influenced by the therapist in a reciprocal relationship. Through acceptance, a therapist is able to convey that their goals are to simply understand the child in a descriptive, nonjudgmental manner, to discover the child's perspective and intentions that are associated with his behavior, and to join him in his experience. When the child is confident that the therapist's primary intention is to understand his intentions, the child is much more likely to openly explore what his intentions are and what his behavior means. With the sense that the therapist "gets it," the child is then likely to be more open to his own perspective and reasons for or concerns about his behavior, if he has any.

Infants repeatedly experience unconditional acceptance from their parents as they develop a secure attachment with them. They come to trust that their parents will act in a way that is in their best interests. In these cases, the intention of the parent is to do what is best for the child. This intention is embedded in a commitment to care for the child no matter what—for better or for worse.

When parents are able to communicate that their child's inner life—their child's thoughts, feelings, wishes, and perceptions—are not being judged, the core experience of acceptance deepens over time. When the parent accepts the inner life of the child even when the parent sets limits on the child's behavior, the child is able to trust the meaning of the limit. The parent is evaluating only the behavior and not the child herself. The child is accepted, even if the behavior is not. This experience strengthens the child's secure attachment because the child trusts that the parent will always remain committed to ensuring the child's safety—regardless of any differences that they have.

The same is true of the child's relationship with the therapist. When the therapist is able to show nonjudgmental interest in the child's inner life—getting to know and accept what the child thinks, feels, wants, values, and perceives—the child is also likely to experience safety while the therapist is exploring the child's challenging behaviors or events that are stressful for the child. The child's sense of shame is activated when the child experiences himself as bad, deficient, or unlikable. When the therapist shows acceptance of the child's inner life, regardless of his specific behaviors, the child's experience of shame is likely to be contained, reduced, or prevented from emerging.

It is important for the therapist to keep in mind that the child is likely to experience the therapist as accepting when the therapist has a conversation with the child about the child's inner life while speaking with a rhythmic and story-telling voice and looking at the child with an open and engaged facial expression. This tends to be easy to do when the conversation is about light, routine, and cooperative experiences. It is more difficult to engage the child in this manner when the content involves conflicts and challenging behaviors. It is crucial that the therapist—and parents—see the value of frequently engaging the child in this manner, regardless of the content being explored. In this way, the child will develop a sense of trust that can contain any conflicts being explored, remain open and engaged with the conversation, and be much less likely to become defensive. She will be better able to revisit the difficulties she is having for what they are, namely, specific challenges that she is facing, not fixed features of herself. The conversation then is likely to continue with a tone of joint, cooperative, exploration and understanding. If the therapist or parent relates with a stern, evaluative monotone, the child is likely to disagree, find excuses, blame others, distort the events, and become angry, all of which are strategies the child may use to reduce their experience of shame. Such overt evaluations of the child, even though they may seem reasonable, are nonetheless likely to create defensiveness, along with anger or withdrawal.

EXAMPLE OF ACCEPTANCE:

CHILD: Say whatever you want! I don't believe you! You don't care what I say, you're only interested in what my parents say!

THERAPIST: You don't feel safe at all with me! It seems to you that I only listen to what your parents tell me and that what you tell me is nonsense! No wonder you don't want to talk with me. If it seems like that to you, it would only be a waste of your time!

CHILD: That's how it is, and you can't make me believe anything different.

THERAPIST: And the more I try to change your mind, the more you'll be sure that you're right. You can't feel good now, sitting with three adults when you don't think any of them really care what you have to say!

By accepting the child's experience, the child is likely to then become less defensive—the therapist's nonjudgmental expressions do not evoke defensiveness—and the child is more likely to become open to the possibility that the therapist might actually value and be interested in understanding the child's perspective.

Through our **CURIOSITY**, expressed without judgment, the child is more likely to become curious himself as to why he may have teased the dog, stole from his friend, or took food from the kitchen and then denied doing it. So often, children do not reflect on their own behaviors, and this is especially true when they experience discomfort about what they do. If they feel some shame over doing something that they know goes against what their parents want them to do, they often do not feel safe enough to wonder about why they did it. Knowing they did something wrong, the child may avoid all reflection and be left with a sense of being "bad," selfish, stupid, or lazy. If they have any sense that having one of these undesirable traits was the reason they did what they did, they will avoid all exploration of their behavior, refuse to discuss it with their parents, and search for a quick excuse or justification for it.

The therapist and parent's nonjudgmental curiosity works to lower the chances that this avoidant, defensive, shame-based, pattern will develop. A light, wondering, rhythmic, question, "I wonder what was going on?" is much more likely to evoke an engaged, exploring response than would a stern, mildly irritable, and clearly judgmental: "Why did you do that!"

If the therapist is able to maintain acceptance in his attitude, the child is likely to experience questions using "why," or "how do you make sense of that," or "how was that affecting you" as coming from a desire to understand, not an effort to convince the child that she was wrong. Questions that convey judgments about the child's being right or wrong will evoke defensiveness, often accompanied by silence or anger. Questions that convey a desire to know the child's inner life, to discover what she thinks or feels or wants, will evoke within the child—who is suddenly less alone—a desire to be known and to know herself better.

EXAMPLE OF CURIOSITY:

THERAPIST: Why do you think you told your dad to leave you alone when he came over and asked how you were doing?

CHILD: I don't know!

THERAPIST: I wonder what was going on . . . I wonder . . . Do you think? . . . Do you think maybe you thought he was going to give you a lecture about the big argument that you just had with your mom?

CHILD: Yeah, why talk to him? He's just going to take her side!

THERAPIST: So did it seem then . . . does it seem a lot . . . that your dad always seems to think that your mom is right and you're wrong?

CHILD: I just said that! He always takes her side!

THERAPIST: And if that's how it feels to you, then you probably don't feel very close to your dad at the same time as you're not feeling close to your mom . . . that would be hard . . . I wonder if it might have been possible that your dad wasn't taking sides then, but rather was just letting you know that he knew you were having a hard time and he wanted to be with you so it might not be so hard . . . Do you think that's possible?

CHILD: Maybe.

THERAPIST: Can we ask him?

CHILD: I guess.

The therapist's curiosity might not lead to new insights in the child at the time that the therapist asks him about his experience. But the therapist's questions often stay with the child and over time create some doubts within the child's negative assumptions. But only when the curiosity is embedded in acceptance. Then the child becomes confident that, as the child and therapist explore the child's inner life, the therapist will not be evaluating what they uncover there. They will not be finding something that the therapist thinks is shameful.

Finally, there is **EMPATHY**, which is crucial in helping children face vulnerable states of sadness, fear, shame, and doubt. Because of the therapist's empathy, the child will not have to handle her vulnerability alone and will more readily address these stressful experiences to resolve them. The adult's empathy is evoked by the child's vulnerability, but only if the adult is able to integrate his own similar states. If the therapist or caregiver tends to avoid and deny their own sadness and fears, they are unlikely to be able to assist the child in facing his. Empathy says to the child "I am with you in your distress, we will handle it together . . . together . . . and you will be safe as we make sense of these events. Because we are together in dealing with them, they will not be too much for you to manage."

EXAMPLE OF EMPATHY

CHILD: I swore at my dad . . . and he looked so mad but he did not say anything. He did not say anything and he left the house and got in the car and left.

THERAPIST: Oh, my! He didn't say anything! And you didn't know . . . what he was going to do.

CHILD: I thought that he was going to give up on me. That he had had enough and he decided I wasn't worth it.

THERAPIST: How hard that must have been . . . if you thought that your dad . . . your dad . . . might be giving up . . . giving up on you . . . how hard . . .

CHILD: (now crying) Why did I have to swear at him! I didn't mean it!

Expressions of empathy tend to evoke feelings of vulnerability and at times the child or teenager does not want to be vulnerable! In these cases, it is best that the therapist express empathy with less emotion in his voice, in a more matter of fact tone, which might evoke less vulnerability and thus be accepted by the child.

The four aspects of PACE are well suited to facilitating the goals of building relational trust while developing both emotional regulation and social cognition, which are central in an attachment-based model of therapy. Playfulness sets a safe and optimistic tone that helps the child to regulate positive emotional experiences while maintaining the momentum of the conversation as it moves through many stressful events. Acceptance greatly contributes to the child's sense of safety and their readiness to enter into a reciprocal relationship that will aid in both emotional regulation and reflective functioning. Curiosity excels at supporting the child's social cognition and, especially, her reflective skills. Empathy helps the child to regulate stressful emotional experiences and at the same time experience the active presence of the therapist so that she knows that she is not alone and is able to experience comfort. Together, both parent and therapist are able to assist the child in experiencing a level of trust in them that enables the child to integrate any stressful event. Together, the qualities of PACE greatly aid in coregulating all emerging emotions while cocreating new meanings of the memories being explored.

AFFECTIVE-REFLECTIVE DIALOGUE

The primary therapeutic activity in DDP is having a conversation, not "just talking." It is a conversation in which the hearts (affective) and minds (reflective) of the therapist and child are jointly engaged in experiencing each other, moment-to-moment, while also experiencing memories of past events in the child's life. We call this affective–reflective dialogue because it combines both feeling and thinking. These are the cornerstones of some of the evidence we reviewed in Chapter 2 that support the developmental value of attachment theory in developing trust, emotional regulation, and reflective function.

Feeling without thinking tends toward catharsis, which is not likely to have lasting value. Thinking without feeling is likely to lead toward intellectualization, which tends to be too light to have an impact on the child's developing experience. Affective–reflective (A–R) dialogues create the sense of a shared activity that is safe and engaging. Their function is to describe, experience, and understand meanings, and through this joint re-experiencing of past events, cocreate new meanings—meanings that can be integrated with less shame and fear than was characteristic of the old meanings.

The characteristics of A–R dialogue will be presented in detail in Chapter 5 in which we explore how to help children to be safe enough to engage in conversations that create trust.

FOLLOW-LEAD-FOLLOW

DDP is neither a directive nor a nondirective model of therapy. The DDP therapist focuses on developing a conversation that integrates the initiatives and responses of both the child and the therapist. The closest analogy is the "serve and return" sequence that characterizes the reciprocal engagement of the parent and infant. The therapist usually invites the child to initiate the focus of the conversation. The therapist works to understand and possibly deepen the content of the theme while also trying to help to integrate it with other events in the child's life. Deepening the theme usually refers to discovering and exploring what lies under the surface behaviors and events. The therapist's curiosity might take the lead: I wonder why? What was that like? How do you make sense that? What does it mean? Is that different than other times? The therapist then leads the conversation into a related theme or a new theme that may have been avoided by the child in his previous initiatives. After leading, the therapist immediately notices the child's response to the lead, and the therapist then follows the child's response. By following the child's focus, the therapist is attending to the child's need for safety as well as to what may be a more important theme to the child at a given moment. Engaging in follow-lead-follow facilitates the child's experience of acceptance, which generates a sense of trust. Following the child's lead ensures emotional regulation. Leading facilitates reflective functioning.

Suppose the child keeps avoiding a theme that seems to be making his life very difficult. The therapist follows the child, accepting the avoidance, and going to another area. Later in the session, or during a later session, the child might easily go into that avoided theme and make sense of it with the therapist's participation. What to do though, when the next time and the time after that, the avoidance is just as strong? The following process might be helpful:

1. Comment on the avoidance with an attitude of acceptance, and acknowledge that some things are hard to talk about, or even remember. Wonder aloud if the child can think of other things that once were hard to talk about but now are not.

2. Share your curiosity about what the child thinks the therapist's motive is for initiating this topic. To convince him that he was wrong? To scold him for what he is doing and for not trying hard enough to stop? To remind his parents of what he has done so that they will become angry with him again? To make him unhappy? To give him coping skills so that he can do something different? To take his parents side and tell them what consequences that they need to give him to get him to change? After the child assents to one or more of those guesses, the therapist expresses understanding and empathy for his wanting to avoid the theme if that's what he thought the therapist's motives were for bringing it up. Following the expression of empathy, the therapist might give information about her motives:

    THERAPIST: I know this has been hard for you and your parents, John. You get angry, they get angry, and then you don't feel very close to each other! And you think they need to change, and they think you need to change! Oh, my, and it then happens again and again, and no one is happy. Everyone gets mad . . . and maybe sad after a bit. And that's why I bring it up! If I can make sense of what's happening for all of you—why it's so hard for all of you to figure it out—and then find something that you all feel good about, I will be very happy . . . very glad that I could help you and your family.

3. The therapist first makes it clear that she accepts that the child does not want to talk about it, and then the therapist explores with the parents their perspectives. The therapist leads the conversation with the parents about the event, ensuring that they are not now expressing anger, not blaming the child by attributing to him poor motives ("He just wants his own way all the time.") feelings ("He's so quick to get angry when we're trying to be reasonable."), or thoughts ("He thinks that he's always right and we're always wrong."). If the parents do start to express negative views about their child, the therapist qualifies or challenges what they are saying:

THERAPIST: It seems to you that your son doesn't want to hear your reasons, he just becomes angry. I wonder if he sometimes feels the same, that you really don't understand why something is that important to him, or that you don't care about what he wants. If he thought that, would you understand why he might get angry?

Or

THERAPIST: So your guess is that he does that to make you angry. And then you get angry! I wonder if you are right about his reasons . . . and if you are right . . . why he would want to make you angry. Do you think that maybe sometimes he feels that if you make him unhappy by saying "no" to him, he'll make you unhappy too?

Or

THERAPIST: Why do you think you get angry when he comes home late? Because you've told him a number of times and he still comes home late? Still, what's under your anger? Do you think that some of your anger is that you worry . . . did something happen this time? Maybe you get scared because you love him so much and you don't want him to get hurt! I wonder if the anger makes that confusing for him, that he doesn't understand your being scared that he might be hurt and you don't know. And that your fears are strong sometimes because your love for him is so strong.

After such efforts to ensure that the parents are communicating with PACE and not anger and judgments, the therapist might turn back to the child. The child might now have some trust that the conversation will not lead to the conclusion that he is wrong or selfish. Rather the conversation will be focused on understanding the child—without judging his thoughts and feelings—and giving him a chance to talk with his parents with some confidence that the therapist will be working to ensure that they listen and understand him, too. By talking to the parents about the theme, the child is able to listen safely in the background. As long as the therapist can ensure that anger and shame-provoking comments are not made by the parents, the child often feels safe enough to join in when invited.

4.   If the therapist has been able to have a successful conversation with the child about things that are not stressful, the child might allow the therapist to speak to his parents for him, guessing what he might be thinking, with the agreement that if the child wants the therapist to stop at any point or to add something that he thinks or feels, that she will do so. This is a safer way for the child to explore the theme: vicariously, with the therapist being the spokesperson for him. The intervention of talking for the child, along with a similar intervention of talking about him, will be explored shortly.

5.   Sometimes, continuing to explore the theme in these less direct ways will not be sufficient to evoke the child's cooperation with the process. In that case, it is wise to postpone

discussing this theme to another session and focus instead on re-engaging the child using another theme that is less stressful.

INTERACTIVE REPAIR

In the 1980s, Ed Tronick, while studying the moment to moment interactions between an infant and his parent, noticed that the infant frequently signaled the parent that he did not enjoy the parent's movements and expressions, and the parent then modified what she was doing. Tronick (2007) called this *interactive repair* to suggest that the parent's change in her engagement with her infant improved the joint expression of the relationship at that moment. Through interactive repair, the relationship became more able to increase the child's sense of safety in his parent's presence, to assist the child in regulating his emotions, and to support the child's attending to something of interest to him. His parent was sensitive to his expressions—his nonverbal communications—and then responded to him. For example, if the parent approached the infant with intense, animated, expressions, and the infant responded by becoming quieter and looking away, the parent then became quieter and gentler in her communications. This was then likely to be followed by the infant becoming re-engaged with the parent, and their communications continued in a way that was more comfortable and synchronized with the infant's needs. Trust develops through repair. Emotion becomes regulated with repair. Internal working models that involve trust and acceptance emerge within relationships in which repair is common.

Synchronization is crucial for the child's sense of safety because it ensures that the therapist is continuously engaged in interactive repair of their moment-to-moment communications and is communicating that the child's wishes are seen and responded to. Too often, therapists avoid addressing something that the child needs to explore for fear that the child will experience the therapist as being intrusive and that the child will feel trapped in the conversation, forced to explore something that is frightening, stressful, or shameful. However, research indicates that active attention to these ruptures fosters engagement and is effective in establishing relationships that can become truly therapeutic (Daly, Llewelyn, McDougall, & Chanen, 2010). Through synchronization of nonverbal communications, the child quickly learns that their wishes, thoughts, and feelings are important and that they are safe because the interactions are being jointly developed. Their communications matter to the therapist! When the therapeutic dialogue is a joint, cooperative activity, the child will experience therapy as a safe activity that will not take them into themes or memories that feel too difficult to explore.

The benefits of interactive repair do not end with infancy; interactive repair is a crucial aspect of maintaining the child's sense of safety with her parent and maintaining the vitality of their relationship for years to come. Through interactive repair the parent signals the child that the relationship is very important and that any time there is a stress on the relationship—separation, conflict, misunderstandings—the parent will communicate to the child how important the relationship is. Although at times this might involve an apology when the parent realizes that he was insensitive to the child, often it is simply an acknowledgment that what just occurred was hard for the child and the parent is available to assist the child in feeling close to the parent again.

EXAMPLE OF INTERACTIVE REPAIR
BETWEEN PARENT AND CHILD

Jenny was gone for three days to visit her mother, who was having some medical problems. Though Jenny had told April (her 8-year-old daughter) how long she would be away and why, and though April's father Steve, who was always quite an active caregiver, remained home, April was somewhat withdrawn from Steve while her mother was gone, and she was fairly irritable when Jenny returned. Jenny thought that April's distress might be related to the separation, but rather than explaining again why she had left and reassuring her that she will always come back, she engaged April with an attitude of PACE, conveying acceptance of April's experience, understanding it, and then connecting with empathy over her distress. Jenny said:

> It seems that it was hard for you while I was gone, and maybe you're still kind of bothered by our not being together. I can understand that. We like to talk in the evening before bed and I wasn't here! And your dad doesn't cook as well as I do. And I think that you missed me. I think that because I know I was missing you. I was sad that I wanted to be with your granny to help her out and that meant that I couldn't be with you. I'm glad that I'm back now and don't think I'll have to visit her again without you for a long time—if ever.

Another example involves interactive repair after an angry conflict between Jake and his son, Robert (age 11). Jake had expressed frustration that Robert had not watched their dog as he said he would, and the dog got loose, and it took a few hours for them to find him. Robert responded angrily that he feels that he is never good enough for his dad. Whenever he is not perfect, his dad is always annoyed with him. After a bit more anger was expressed, Robert left the kitchen for his bedroom. After Jake calmed himself, reflected a bit, and thought that Robert would probably be a bit calmer too, he went to Robert's room.

> Hi. How are you? We both got kind of angry there didn't we? We both probably said some things that might have been kind of hard for the other to hear. Times like this are hard for me because we're not very close now and I really enjoy the times when we are close, do stuff together, and talk about everything! And we're not there right now. In fact, you're feeling that I want you to be perfect and don't really feel good about you if you make a mistake. That must really be hard for you, if that's how it seems to you. It makes me think that I'm not doing a good job of showing you how much I love you and that I am so proud of you as my son. I have to find a better way of showing you that so that when we do argue again, you'll still know how glad I am to be your father.

Interactive repair is also very important to maintain the therapeutic relationship between the therapist and all members of the family. It is of great value for the therapist to initiate repair when the child—or parent—experiences the therapist as judgmental or insensitive.

EXAMPLE OF INTERACTIVE REPAIR BETWEEN THERAPIST AND FAMILY MEMBERS

THERAPIST (TO PARENT): What would you say is the hardest part for you of his refusing to do what you tell him to do?

PARENT: Are you saying that I shouldn't be angry about that? That I should just be ok about his defying me?

THERAPIST: I'm sorry that what I said made you think that I think that you should not get angry over his defiance of you! That's not what I meant at all—I must have said it poorly.

Others might question why the therapist apologized to the parent if she believed that she asked a reasonable question, expressed appropriately. Because that was not the parent's experience of the question! The parent experienced it as a negative criticism of him, which most likely undermined his sense of safety. Others might say that the parent may be projecting onto the therapist past criticisms from another relationship. While that might be accurate, it is still not the parent's experience. If this happened a number of times, the therapist might wonder about a possible pattern in the parent's response and, if the parent agreed, how they might make sense of it. And if the parent became defensive about the question of a pattern, again, the therapist might be wise to repair the relationship by indicating that was not her intention to criticize the parent. Over the course of these dialogues in which repair occurs over and over again, the parent develops trust in the therapist and her intentions toward the family.

The same would apply to the therapist's relationship with the child:

THERAPIST: So if I understand it right, you were not allowed to use your phone because you hadn't finished what you had told your dad you would do?

CHILD: Yeah, right, I've heard it all before! You think that I'm lazy just like my dad does! You think that I never handle my responsibilities and just want to fool around!

THERAPIST: I'm sorry, John, that I said that in a way that made you think that I think you're lazy. If I thought that, of course you wouldn't trust me enough to tell me what was going on, because you probably think I wouldn't believe you anyway!

Once the child's experience is accepted and understood and the child's defensiveness is much less and he is open and engaged again, then the therapist might wonder if the child has similar experiences with others (his parents especially).

SPEAKING FOR AND SPEAKING ABOUT

A central goal of DDP is to have conversations involving the parent, child, and therapist. In our review of the research in Chapter 2, we have seen that secure relationships demonstrate greater degrees of reflective function (the expression of one's intentions and one's reflections on the minds of others). These conversations will be therapeutic only when they occur within a developing sense of trust and an open and engaged attitude. When the content involves difficult themes, such as the child's behaviors, parent–child conflicts, or other relationship stresses, the child often will have difficulty engaging in the conversation. This may relate to her not having the words to express her inner life or her not wanting to use the words she has for fear of being criticized or rejected by her parents. The therapist takes an active stance of interceding when a member of the family becomes defensive and angry. Remaining open and engaged himself, the therapist goes under the family member's anger to evoke their vulnerability or positive intentions about what is being explored. Often the therapist does so by speaking for or speaking about the child (or parent).

Speaking for or speaking about often contributes to the therapeutic value of the conversation for various reasons:

1. The therapist makes explicit the vulnerability or intentions that the child was unable or unwilling to say to his parents.

2. The child feels much safer when the therapist speaks for him than when he has to speak for himself.

3. When speaking for the child, the therapist expresses the vulnerability with the associated nonverbal affective expressions that tend to evoke similar vulnerability in the child as well as empathy for the child from the parent.

4. When speaking for the child, the therapist makes the child's experience explicit and then directs the parent to respond to the experience with PACE, not with reasons, arguments, or reassurance.

5. When speaking about the child, the therapist always speaks of the vulnerable or positive intentions related to the child's behavior, never speaking about the child in a critical manner.

6. Often when the therapist speaks about the child, the child listens more openly and tends to believe what the therapist is saying to a greater extent than if the therapist were speaking directly to the child.

7. When the therapist speaks about the child to the parents, the therapist is conveying her experience of the child in a way that tends to elicit from the parents a similar experience. It helps the parents to step out of what may be a habitual negative perception of the child and open up to a new way of experiencing him.

EXAMPLE OF SPEAKING FOR

In this example the therapist and the child had successfully explored and developed the thoughts and feelings that led to the child's behavior, in which he had refused to talk with his parents for the past 24 hours. With the child's permission, the therapist then spoke for the child about the event and his thoughts and feelings, with the understanding that the child would correct her if she was inaccurate.

> **THERAPIST (SPEAKING FOR CHILD TO PARENT):** I didn't talk to you—I know that! I was so mad I thought that it would only get worse if I told you what was going on inside! . . . It seems to me . . . it seems to me . . . you NEVER let me do what I want to do! LIKE WHAT I WANT IS NOT IMPORTANT TO YOU! . . . Like I'm not important to you. So I didn't want to talk to you. I wanted you to know what I feel like . . . I wanted to show you that you're not important to me either . . . but you are . . . you are important . . . but . . . I sometimes don't want you to be so much. (The last four phrases said more and more quietly, with distress.)

> **PARENT:** Oh, Mike, now I understand! You felt that what you want is not important to me . . . and that you even are not important to me. No wonder you were angry with me. It would have been so hard to think that you're not important to me . . . and you are important to me . . . so very, very important . . . but you didn't feel that . . . you didn't know that.

The therapist would have explored with the parent in a prior session the importance of responding with PACE when the therapist talks for their child. The parent is being asked not to disagree with their child's experience, but to accept and understand their experience and respond with empathy. When parents feel safe with the therapist, they very often respond well to such direct guidance.

EXAMPLE OF SPEAKING ABOUT

This therapist had been facilitating a difficult conversation about a recent conflict between a teenager, Ken, and his parents. Ken expressed anger while saying that it was hopeless, and then refused to continue his conversation with the therapist. The parents showed some frustration and the therapist anticipated that they were about to express disappointment in Ken for no longer talking. The therapist turned to the parents and said:

> **THERAPIST:** I think that we need to understand how hard this is now for Ken . . . to tell us how bothered he is over what happened . . . while not having confidence that anything will change . . . And I sense you might be starting to get a bit impatient . . . and I need to tell you that Ken is doing the best that he can now. We all have to be patient with this process of having a conversation about this hard stuff . . . my sense is that you all have not had much success at it at home, though I think that you've all tried . . . the anger sometimes gets too big for one or more of you . . . and with anger . . . it's just hard to put what we are feeling inside into words . . . so hard.

After a bit of silence, the therapist turned back to Ken and gently asked what it is like to feel so hopeless. Ken responded with vulnerability about how he sometimes feels that he's ruining the family and he's tried to change but doesn't think he can.

When, as a therapist, you speak for a child or speak about a child to his parents (or even speaking about the child to yourself—thinking out loud), you are actively engaged in making explicit your guesses about the child's mind. About the child's thoughts, feelings, wishes, and perceptions. This facilitates the child's ability to begin to do it for himself. You are his "spokesperson" when he does not have the words—when he does not know what his reflections are. Often, over the course of DDP, the child gradually speaks more and more openly and clearly for herself and there is no value or need for the therapist to continue as spokesperson. The child has developed the reflective functioning skills needed to do it herself. The child is empowered to speak for herself!

This active process—if it is to be therapeutic and indeed attachment informed—needs continuous monitoring with follow-lead-follow and interactive repair to ensure that the therapist's guesses about the mind of the child are on target. If they are not, you try another guess or invite the child to express what is more accurate. Just as the qualities of reflective function and social cognition permit inquiry but no certainty about the mind of the other, so it is here. Often the child's nonverbal expressions demonstrate whether your guesses are "good enough" or if they are not accurate in one way or another. If the child's response is ambiguous, then you need to explicitly ask him if your guess is accurate or not. If the child says that it is not, you must always accept his view about his inner life and never try to impose your view. He needs to trust that you fully accept him even if he disagrees with you. Like other initiatives that you make as a therapist, speaking for and speaking about require the presence of interactive repair to maintain the child's sense of safety and the integrity of the therapeutic intervention.

SUMMARY

Without trust, there can be no sense of safety. PACE is an excellent way to incorporate what we know about successful secure relationships and to communicate a deep interest in and acceptance of the inner life of the child. If the child experiences unconditional acceptance regarding her thoughts, feelings, ideas, perceptions, and wishes, the child is likely to trust that you, her therapist, and his parents are truly interested in getting to know who she is. She will then be in a better place to explore difficulties and the ideas of those who are seeking to help her. If you or her parents then have any concerns about her behavior, these can be addressed safely because the child herself is not bad, stupid, or lazy. There is room for behavioral differences or challenges if the value of the child and of the relationship are not in question. Trusting that she is safe, both with regard to the sense of self and also in the importance of the relationship, the child is then safe to explore any challenges that need to be addressed. This is the foundation for all successful and engaged therapeutic interactions. The five components we have described here are akin to those elements shown to be effective across psychotherapies, as we discussed in the Introduction (Norcross & Wampold, 2018), which can be incorporated into your practice.

These components may be integrated into the treatment goals and interventions of other therapies. This is because these five aspects offer a solid foundation for engagement and mutual purpose which, once established, will increase the ability of other interventions to be shared and learned from. The organizing principles of DDP develop and maintain an open and engaged attitude, which is necessary for developing integrative conversations around the themes that have brought the family for treatment. As the therapist, you explore these themes from a developmental perspective, seeing how they might be affected by insecure attachment patterns that may or may not include maltreatment. With the child's parents safely and actively involved in the therapy, they can develop their own attachment-based ways of engagement that will carry over into their daily life. You need to invite the parents to discover ways of developing and maintaining their child's trust in them, regardless of their differences and conflicts, while also seeing how they can assist their child to regulate his emotions and develop internal working models based on reciprocal understanding and influence. The next chapter will explore in greater detail the parent's role in an attachment-based therapy.

chapter four

The Role of the Parent or Caregiver

Working with parents is integral to an attachment informed approach given what we know about attachment and its role in the life of the child. The work with the child effectively begins here. The aim of DDP in working with parents is threefold. DDP seeks to:

1. explore the nature of the difficulties the parent may have in the relationship with their child (how safe they feel in the relationship);
2. explore the origins of these difficulties;
3. improve their capacity for emotional regulation and social cognition and thus with their child.

While we can have some confidence that the attachment security of the parent predicts whether the child will have a secure or an insecure pattern (van IJzendoorn, 1995), research is yet to identify what fully explains this relationship. We discussed this briefly in Chapter 2 when we referred to the "transmission gap". If the parent's attachment is only broadly associated with the child's attachment, what is the focus in DDP as an attachment informed model of therapy? In DDP we are not explicitly seeking to change the attachment status of a parent or the child. Though this may occur and more research is needed, this is not the primary aim. Instead, DDP takes the developmental view of the effects on the parent and child due to insecure attachment and how the effects of the insecure attachment relate to the mental health of the child. In Chapter 2, we reviewed research that indicates that secure attachment in the child enhances emotional regulation and social cognition, important developmental outcomes that permit one to develop trust and successful relationships. Both emotional regulation and social cognition may reduce the likelihood of mental health difficulties and are probably depleted in people with mental health difficulties. And it is these qualities of secure attachment, if they are found wanting in the parent, that DDP seeks to address and work directly with. In working with parents, DDP fosters engaging conversations, emotional regulation, and social cognition in the parent, which should improve the same capacities in their child. This is facilitated by the therapist providing the parent with those qualities associated with secure attachment, giving them first-hand experience of an emotionally regulated, reflective, and safe relationship. This is called the *therapeutic alliance*. It is from here that the development of the child's capacities in these areas can grow to develop resilience and foster well-being.

Therefore, it follows that if we are not explicitly seeking to change the attachment security of the parent, we need an informed, clinically useful understanding of the role of safety and trusting relationships, emotional regulation, and the features of social cognition in parents. The model of blocked care (Hughes & Baylin, 2012) offers a sound, developmental and brain-based understanding of how the parent's capacity for nondefensive relationships, regulation, and social cognition is affected when they find themselves feeling stressed and unsafe. Of course, an insecure attachment history may be one way in which the parent feels unsafe, but the benefit of the blocked care model is that it allows us to reach beyond this history and have more sympathy for how stress on any parent can compromise the qualities even of a secure relationship with their child. Life happens. Stresses, strains, and losses can affect a parent who might otherwise have been doing well enough in terms of attachment. For example, the mistrust of an insecure child who has moved into a foster home may overwhelm even the most secure and capable foster parent. During bereavement from an important attachment figure, a parent's capacity to remain open to the attachment needs of their children may be compromised; particularly if this loss is traumatic due to their preoccupation with their own sense of safety. The blocked care model is a clinically useful tool because it does not require the classification of the adult's attachment status, which otherwise would require a formal and more lengthy measurement, potentially beyond most typical out-patient settings. Instead, blocked care can be formulated using observation, interview, and brief measurements of stress and well-being. Our priority is to help the parent provide the best developmental environment for their child so that the child's mental health difficulties can be addressed fully. We do this by applying the same five components, as appropriate, to the parent as we outlined applying to the child. In this way, developmental outcomes for the child are enhanced by the therapist's provision of the features of secure attachment to the parent (the therapeutic alliance) and then to the parent and child together.

In this chapter, we explain the rationale for work with parents and outline the model of blocked care, giving guidance on how to recognize and assess it in the clinic. We provide a case scenario to illustrate how this work may unfold. In the chapters that follow, we will detail the way the five components of DDP foster emotional regulation and social cognition in the parent, including principles for parenting that may be shared with parents to facilitate bringing home the attachment-based interactions that occur in the office.

Now, let us return to the clinic, a client before us:

MOTHER (PARENT-ONLY SESSION ABOUT HER NINE-YEAR-OLD SON WITH CONDUCT PROBLEMS): A bad week.

THERAPIST: A bad week?

MOTHER: A bad week. The continual lying, faking tears, and the downright mess of it all . . . a bad life more like.

THERAPIST: That's hard . . . hard for you to be a parent to . . .

MOTHER (CUTS THERAPIST OFF): Hard? HARD? He's doing it on purpose. I know he can control it. He can be as nice as . . . then BANG! Fake. Lie. Fake.

THERAPIST: Ah! You're telling me that it would be hard if he couldn't control himself! But it worse than that . . . he seems to do it on purpose! Seems so difficult to know how to be a mother to him.

MOTHER: I just don't know what I am doing. I don't know if he loves me even. I can't see it. I can't see the point of this . . . when is he going to come and face up to things?

THERAPIST: (matching the vitality of the mother's affect and conveying acceptance) You so much want to feel love with your son . . . and his actions make you doubt whether he even does love you! And you're wondering how this is going to change by coming here. . .

MOTHER: Yes! I don't know what he needs, why he does it. He could have a nice life laid out for him, though maybe not now. I'm losing it . . . I shout. He sees me . . . he doesn't see the best of me. Not anymore. I can't do it. I don't feel it.

THERAPIST: You're are in such pain and you are feeling pushed away, and you are questioning what you mean to him because what he is doing is seems so hard to understand, to see why it would be like that, and you find yourself doing things which you regret . . . and make you feel bad as a parent.

At first glance, without even meeting the child, one could easily see that there are struggles for this parent that would impact their child. These include:

- Difficulties remaining close or wanting to be close to the child
- A low sense of reward in the relationship
- Being uncertain about their parental role in the relationship
- Problems understanding the behaviors of the child
- Moments of emotional distress and behavioral dysregulation in the presence of the child

These are difficulties that may reflect a condition called *blocked care* (Hughes & Baylin, 2012). Research in the field of attachment includes studies that delve deep into the neurobiology of attachment and parenting. The blocked care model synthesizes these findings and offers ways to understand the relevance of attending to the needs of the parent so we may assist their child in a way that is informed by attachment theory. Blocked care identifies five interacting parenting systems underpinned by neurobiological pathways and neuroendocrinological mechanisms. We will not detail the neurobiology of parenting in this chapter, but the interested reader is encouraged to read the full story of this fascinating work and research in *Brain-Based Parenting: The Neuroscience of Caregiving for Healthy Attachment*, by Hughes & Baylin (2012). The five parenting systems identified by blocked care are:

1. *Social approach system:* The capacity to remain close and to move toward the distress of the child rather than away
2. *Reward system:* The capacity to enjoy parenting and being with the child
3. *Meaning making system:* The narrative of what it means to be a parent and what it means to parent *this* child
4. *Child reading system:* The capacity to read beneath the behavior to see the emotions and motivations of the child
5. *Executive system:* The capacity to monitor the input from the other parenting systems, regulate the emotions arising from the parenting task at hand, and provide repair. This system enables a parent to continue to care for their child and prevents them from abusing or abandoning their child even when the other systems have shut down. This system helps recover the other systems in the short term moment of high stress. However, if this system has been working hard for a prolonged period, the parent's heart will not seem to be engaged in their caring. Parents may find themselves just "doing their job."

By way of illustration, these five systems mirror the behaviors (in the same order), we listed and identified in the opening example above. When these systems are present and "online," stress is low or well regulated, and the parent will feel safe in the relationship with the child. In the absence of such relational safety, by which we mean the parent is moving or has moved into automatic defensive responses to the child due to stress, these systems go "offline" and the connection with the child is lost. In these circumstances, the parent is preoccupied with finding their own safety. This is what is called blocked care.

Suffice it to say, the higher the number on this list of systems, the higher into the cortical regions of the brain that are engaged. Furthermore, as this journey begins, we also meet some old friends from our first two chapters, social cognition (reflective functioning, internal working models) and emotional regulation; these are associated with the frontal lobes and have connectivity back to the stress response, potentially allowing the frontal lobes to override the amygdala's response, turning off the tendency to move away defensively. Of significance, these frontal regions of the brain and their connectivity to the stress response may be changed throughout the life span by all experiences, notably those characteristic of a secure attachment (Siegel, 2012). Indeed, as reported in van IJzendoorn (1995):

> A trusted friend, spouse, or therapist can provide a "secure base" for exploring and working through adverse childhood experiences and can enable the adult to "earn" a coherent and autonomous attachment representation. (p. 339)

Let us return to the brain. There are more immediate and direct links with the stress response in the limbic system. This drives the social approach system, triggering the approach or avoid instinct, and also underpins the reward system, which reflects how good it feels to be in the relationship. Together this is where the core parental emotions of joy and the pathway to move toward the emotional needs of the child.

Further up the brain, we move into the systems associated

with memory that provide a person's "felt sense" and their sense of relationships. These will be familiar to us as internal working models. In here is where the story they hold about themselves as a person who has entered a new relationship in their life is stored, this time as a parent (parent meaning making system). As we have seen, this is formed by early attachment relationships and the layers of experiences and behaviors in relationships, including with their child, that may maintain or challenge these templates.

Beyond this, still further up toward the frontal regions of the brain, we meet another old companion: the role of reflective functioning. As a developmental outcome of secure attachment, reflective functioning is seen in the capacity for reading the emotions of the child (child reading system).

Managing these systems, and overriding stress if there is the capacity, is the executive system. This is another associated friend of attachment. The executive system involves the capacity for emotional regulation in the parent when faced with stress and can help organize and call the other parenting systems to order.

So as we go up through the brain, integration through connectivity between the parenting systems becomes more crucial. If a lower system is overridden by stress, we might expect the others to close down or never be reached at all unless the executive system can be called into play. Just as the development of the child to regulate and reflect is a function of attachment security, so we may see the same capacity in the parent as reflecting their attachment experiences in their formative years.

ASSESSING BLOCKED CARE

When assessing the parent's needs and the presence of blocked care in the clinic, it is helpful to attend to the well-being of the parent. A check in about their health, well-being, and lives is a simple way to establish a dialogue about their needs. Indeed, insecure attachment patterns are overrepresented in child clinic samples if we consider the role of maternal well-being (van IJzendoorn, Goldberg, Kroonenberg, and Frenkel (1992). Attention to the well-being of the parent is important if we are to consider the same for their child. Understanding parenting stress and the stressors the parents live with is sometimes overlooked in standard mental health interviews when the focus is on the child and their presenting problems. There may be health issues or conditions that have a bearing on one's parenting capacity, such as disability or head injury. These organic causes need to be considered.

We propose that from the moment of meeting the parent, attention to the five components, PACE, interactive repair, and the principle of follow-lead-follow are necessary to assist our understanding of the person before us. We will say more later in this chapter about the importance of providing parents with secure attachment experiences to bring them into better regulation and reflection during our time with them.

As part of this process, measures of parenting stress, anxiety, or depression may be useful screens for general levels of parental stress and/or distress. If these are of concern, they can be considered "red flags" for possible blocked care that require our closer attention and connection. But to understand each of the parenting systems, it may be helpful to ask parents the following additional questions:

Are there times when your child is distressed that you move away from them due to your own feelings? (Social approach system)

Are there times when you lack joy with your child? Are there times when you can enjoy their company? (Reward system)

What does it mean to be a parent to your child? How has the experience of becoming a parent changed you? What impact has it had on your outlook on life? (Parent meaning making system)

When your child is challenging your ability to manage, what are they feeling? What needs are they trying to meet through that behavior? (Child reading system)

Are there times when you struggle to manage and control your emotions? Do you behave in ways that either surprise you and/or concern you? Are there extended periods of time that the best you can do is simply "do your job" without your heart being engaged? (Executive system)

If we find that there are struggles for the parent in each of these domains, or in some of them, we can move toward understanding the origins of the blocked care. There are four origins of blocked care: 1) chronic blocked care, 2) acute blocked care, 3) stage-specific blocked care, and 4) child-specific blocked care. As we discuss each of these, we highlight broad areas for inquiry that may help formulate the pattern before you. If we do expand our practice this way, it moves us closer to formulating with them the origins of their parenting struggles, if present. Stress that overwhelms the parenting systems and leads to blocked care may be traceable to one or more of four origins:

CHRONIC BLOCKED CARE

Unresolved trauma from the parent's childhood. In these circumstances, the parent rarely reaches the capacity for any of the parenting systems to turn on. Instead, they may be more preoccupied with their own sense of safety and even experience the relationship with the child as a source of danger. If we hear that there have consistently been difficulties in the parent–child relationship since birth, we may wish to steer our interviews toward an understanding of the parent's attachment history. We may wish to ask how their parents responded to them when they needed comfort as children. Siegel and Hartzell (2003) have developed some questions to help the parent understand the impact of their attachment history has had on them. We weave some of these questions into the examples of dialogue later in the chapter. It is important to note not just what parents tell us in these interviews. How coherent they are in their language when they answer can give us a sense of whether the experiences they describe are unresolved, but in a much less formal way than the Adult Attachment Interview would use to code classifications. For example, this may include paying particular attention to unfinished sentences when there is an apparent interruption of language due to strong feelings about the experience for the parent.

The other three origins typify specific circumstances by which stress takes parenting offline for a period of time.

ACUTE BLOCKED CARE

When the attachment system of the parent is activated due to loss or illness, the capacity to regulate stress may be reduced. Seemingly well-functioning parenting patterns may start to diminish. Our assessing interviews should include whether there have been any changes, such as those characterized by loss (possibly of a job), or illness or a move to another city, that may be impacting the parent's well-being.

STAGE-SPECIFIC BLOCKED CARE

Stress related to developmentally typical separations. When children are developmentally capable of exploring the world themselves, they move further away from the physical presence of the parent. There are two such stages seen in typically developing children: 1) from baby to toddler and 2) from child to adolescent. Both involve a degree of exploration that stretches the relationship with the parent who must negotiate the child's exploration with safety (how close they are). But the world is full of risks: For the toddler, this is the sharp-edged table as they teeter around the room. For the adolescent, it is the temptation of novelty and risk that complicate driving and pique their interest in trying alcohol and drugs. These can be stressful times in the development of the child and may overwhelm some parents. For some parents, infancy itself presents many challenges for the parent, whereas their caregiving is satisfactory throughout the following stages. Knowing the age and stage of the child may help the therapist understand what is most stressful for the parent. Asking questions to determine whether the parent's stress is in response to current circumstances or it has always been present will reveal whether the origin of the blocked care is stage-specific or chronic.

CHILD-SPECIFIC BLOCKED CARE:

Stress associated with the attachment profile or pattern of needs in the child. Due to the specific natures of the parent and the child pairing, there may be behaviors that "press emotional buttons" of the parent. This may include when the child rejects comfort from the parent. There may also be something about the child's characteristics and behavior—the way they look, speak, or behave—that reminds the parent of a previous relationship, characterized by fear or distress. Some parents find providing care for their very active child challenging, while other parents find relating to their inhibited or shy child challenging. This is different from chronic blocked care, in which all relationships seem to trouble the parent. This blocked care may be caused by the child's pattern of attachment, which may confound the persistent provision of care and nurturing if such provisions are consistently rejected by the child. This characteristic is common in foster or adopted children with very insecure attachment profiles and who turn *away* from others for comfort. Understanding the child's profile of needs in relationships, including their pattern of security, can be especially helpful here. If there are other children in the family, is there evidence of the same difficulties with them? What is it about this child that, for this parent, causes the struggle?

Might we expect there to be important differences in how we approach the parent depending on these patterns? There may be. Chronic and child-specific blocked are much more likely where attachment difficulties are present for the parent and also probably for the child. More attention to the building of the alliance will probably be needed because regulation and reflectivity will be lower. Acute and stage-specific blocked care may reflect parenting that has previously been adequate but is now under some stress. Attending to the therapeutic alliance will be helpful, but other interventions associated with stress management will also be useful here. Acute and stage-specific blocked care often present because the executive system has broken under the strain of the stressor; restoring this may produce a renewal in parenting capabilities. These other interventions include mindfulness based cognitive therapy, which we will discuss in the final chapter of this book.

By giving time to the relationship with the parent, we will be able to mentalize the parent-child relationship for the parent so that they can understand the model of their own mind as well as that of their child's mind. We will also know what may dysregulate the parent, what creates the parents' defensiveness, and how best to enable them to become open and engaged during the session with or without their child present. This level of

understanding will be helpful not only when thinking about
the relationship in sessions with the child but also by forming a
therapeutic alliance with the parent—it will help parents know
their parenting mind better, too. Parents will feel safer to repair
and reconnect with us; there will be what we call a therapeutic
alliance. This is a primary objective in working with parents in
an attachment informed approach.

BUILDING THE THERAPEUTIC ALLIANCE WITH PARENTS

POTENTIAL PITFALLS AND ROADBLOCKS

In order to work with the triad of the child's capacity for trust,
reflection, and regulation, we will first need to assist parents to
be able to be close to their child's experiences of themselves and
others with the same qualities. Jon Baylin refers to this as developing a "round view" of their children—a three-dimensional
model of the whole child. If the parent has a "flat view" of
their child, they make automatic, one-dimensional sense of their
children, seeing only the behavior and not much else behind
it such as the child's feelings or the child's view of themselves.
This can lead them to the trap of only using consequences (e.g.,
sanctions or punishments) to change the child's behavior that
is causing the parent the distress. For the parent in a state of
blocked care, this appears to be the only solution. They want
the pain gone. As quickly as possible. When these do not work,
they may increase the severity of the consequence in a desper-
ate bid to have some influence on the behavior and without
success they may develop a rigid view of the child as being bad
and also rejecting of them. Hughes & Baylin (2012) describe
the parent who only has a preoccupation with the behaviour

can show a *heightened focus on consequences*. This may be a useful cue to us that the parent is in blocked care. The tragedy here is that by ignoring the systems associated with the child's capacity for developing safety and trust, reflective functioning, and regulation this limits opportunities to influence the child's behavior successfully. It may also maintain the blocked care because it does not engage the systems that underpin recovery and learning. That is, the systems of trust, safety, regulation and reflectivity in the child which, when present, would mean the parent experiences a child who is receptive to them. When regulated and feeling safe, the child is able to listen and learn from the parent and becomes more rewarding, reciprocal, and joyful to parent. As Jon Baylin states, defense leads to mutual defense. Children are less able to learn from their behavior if they are feeling anxious, unsafe, and full of shame. In a state of shame, they are unable to evaluate their behavior fully until they understand that they are safe and that they are not a "bad child." If the parent can move the child out of feeling shame, by showing to the child that *they* feel safe by being regulated and reflective themselves, they can convey a more effective message to change the behavior. The child will know that yes, they did something wrong, but the parent is safe and ready to support them with it. In the beginning stages of working with parents, they may present with an urgent expectation of solutions and strategies. This is why they are here after all! They are in distress about their child. They may well have good intentions that they hope their child behaves better even though they react with criticism, harshness, and defensiveness to their child. They may have waited a long time to be helped. This scenario may tempt the therapist to provide these to reduce the distress of the parent, but without PACE for the parent's distress, this will potentially move the interaction away from a secure interaction to one that escalates dysregulation and reduces reflective functioning. Take this example of a brief interaction *without* PACE:

> **PARENT:** I want answers! Tell me what to do with him! It's a nightmare!
>
> **THERAPIST:** Ok, that sounds difficult. Maybe first you need to get some stickers to reward the good behavior you want to see.
>
> **PARENT:** Don't tell me what to do. Done that. I've got the t-shirt.
>
> **THERAPIST:** OK. [Silence]. So, what has worked before?
>
> **PARENT:** If something had worked before, I wouldn't be here, would I?

Without PACE, we may find ourselves down a trap door that closes behind us and the potential for for trust, regulation, and reflection goes with it. Parents struggling in the relationship with their child need to have their feelings accepted and to receive empathy for their "battles." Curiosity and playfulness assist with the development of understanding and keep the journey of the therapeutic alliance flexible and light enough to keep the parent regulated. Let us rerun that scenario again, injecting *some* PACE:

> **PARENT:** I want answers! Tell me what to do with him!
>
> **THERAPIST:** Of course, you are at a loss! You're stuck. [ACCEPTANCE]
>
> **PARENT:** Right!
>
> **THERAPIST:** I'm so sorry that being with your son feels like this. [ACCEPTANCE & EMPATHY]

PARENT: I'm just so tired of it. Sad about it. [EMOTION REGULATES]

THERAPIST: Yes, sad. I wonder *how* being his parent makes you feel sad? [CURIOSITY]

PARENT: Like I'm no good at it. A father failure. An FF!

THERAPIST: That bad. An FF. Who has no answers and feels they are no good. [ACCEPTANCE] You even have an acronym [small PLAYFULNESS]

PARENT: Yeah, though the "f" could stand for something else! [Laughs]

THERAPIST: Yes, but I'm not sure I'd be writing that down in my notes after. [PLAYFULNESS]

PARENT: Yes, you'd be in trouble!

With some PACE, the interaction regulates and the therapeutic alliance deepens. Playfulness early in the relationship may need to be small; after all, we are seeking to develop a relationship that conveys mutual understanding and trust. But taking the opportunity for a small bit of playfulness, as it was here, can lighten the emotional load and provide some relief before moving deeper into the difficulties. Utilizing PACE will allow the understanding of the parent's need to remain regulated as PACE fosters a reflective view of the relationship and their contribution to it.

Without a three-dimensional view of their child, the attachment system of the child will have no home in that relationship. Without a home that can receive and decode the signals of insecurity where present, the child's opportunity for developmental recovery in ongoing trust, emotional regulation, and social cognition weakens and shrinks. For a parent who can develop a round view of their child, being able to regulate and mentalize the relationship will increase in trust while reducing the defensiveness and stress of the child. The role of the therapist is to help the parent develop a round view of their child by experiencing first-hand from the therapist a relationship that promotes safety, reflectivity, and regulation using the five core components.

As for the child with an insecure attachment and emotional and behavior difficulties, parents presenting with their child may come across as defensive and closed to examining their own contribution to any difficulties. They may expect advice and criticism from us. Much of which they have probably heard before. Imagine that as you drive your car along the road, your passenger is critical of your driving. That is hard. But now imagine someone doing the same type of thing but this time as your parent. Ouch! If parents knew that much of what they feel they have been doing wrong is rooted in their efforts to protect themselves, they can begin to move into a nonblaming, less shameful place in the relationship with their child. Sharing a formulation of the blocked care model can be an important first step in empowering them to be different in ways they probably aspire to be different. If this enables parents to reduce their defensiveness while also increasing their open and engaged responsivity, the therapeutic alliance is likely to blossom.

Sometimes, statements and feelings from the parent that typify blocked care can overwhelm the therapist. This can represent a potential roadblock to the development of the therapeutic alliance. Therapists will hear statements about the behavior of parents that go against common, cultural notions of parenting. We may notice we are moved to negative judgments about the parent as the "bigger person in the room." If this happens we may find ourselves empathizing more readily with the child. In these moments, our sense of safety is lost, too. *We* may be in a temporary state of blocked care, as it were. In this way, we may not *enjoy* (reward system) working with the parent. We may experience a heart sinking feeling as we look down our calendar for the day and see we have them scheduled to come during our lunch break. We may find it difficult to *read* (reading system) what is beneath their behavior, and we may lose sight of their aspirations and hopes, which are masked by worrisome reactions to their children. We, too, may find ourselves experiencing spikes in *emotion* (executive system) during sessions, perhaps feeling some shame that we are not really being helpful and wishing we could *move away* (social approach system) somehow from working with this family.

If we do not have a way to understand these moments, our lack of relational safety will be communicated to the parent. This may lead to interactions that lack the elements we are seeking to enhance, such as trust, emotional regulation, and reflection. There may be times of rupture, which need repair. But if we are to be helpful, we will need to establish the same degree of safety for the parent as we do the child. Indeed, we will learn more and know more if we can restore safety. This includes feeling safe enough to face situations that need to be "called out" to enlist the help of other agencies for the welfare and safety of the child. Indeed, by attending to relational safety, we may facilitate this safety in a way that does not leave the parent and child with further experiences that confirm their sense of incompetence or entrench their feelings of shame. The five components we outlined in Chapter 3 will help develop the capacity for exploration and change in the parent as well as give the therapist a route to safety when experiencing a roadblock of this kind.

SAFETY FIRST;
STRATEGIES WILL ARISE

As with some models of attachment-informed treatment, DDP does not, first and foremost, set out to teach parents. Instead, if the qualities of trust, emotional regulation, and reflective functioning are low in the parent, DDP helps the parent develop these through firsthand experience with the therapist. This felt experience, the therapeutic alliance, is achieved through the provision of the five components. Once felt and experienced sufficiently for the parent to show these qualities toward themselves and their child, it is possible that the parent may more readily learn, share, practice, and use skills based on DDP principles or other useful models. We suspect that for the parent with chronic blocked care, significant attention to their relational safety will be needed before they can apply behavioral principles in-the-moment with their children. We need to consider the wellness of the parent first. Indeed there is some evidence that depression in the parent is associated with poorer parent training program outcomes (Harrington et al., 2000) and that unresolved attachment in the parent leads to poorer outcomes of parenting groups that focus solely on behavioral strategies and do not address the attachment needs of the parent (Routh, Hill, Steele, Elliott, & Dewey, 1995).

In the chapters to come, we will outline the principles and skills parents can learn when they feel safe enough. They will be covered in the chapters on engaging in reciprocal conversations, developing emotional regulation, and developing reflective functioning. But as a highlight, these may be understanding PACE, the principles of connection before correction, and the two hands of discipline. In the early stages, training parents is very much a case of helping them feel and experience things first, before strategies are identified and implemented. Indeed, ideas and strategies often arise naturally, in a cocreated way, once the therapeutic alliance is established. This can be a challenge for those who want quick answers or for whom these principles run counter to their own parenting experiences. For example, research shows that adoptive parents who experienced DDP described at first some anxiety because the approach to parenting an insecure child ran counter to commonly held notions of discipline which might work for a secure child (Wingfield & Gurney-Smith, 2018). For example, it shows that staying with acceptance of their child's feelings, particularly about the child's feelings about themselves, was new to them, as they would have ordinarily moved to minimize their child's distress with reassurance rather than staying close, with empathy, for their child's difficult feelings about their lives (Wingfield & Gurney-Smith, 2018). According to the research, providing acceptance to parents in these moments not only models the approach but also helps them regulate their feelings and those of their child, which improve over time (Wingfield & Gurney-Smith, 2018).

Parents may also benefit from learning these principles, which they will use with their child, in a group with other parents. The role of DDP informed parenting courses are also discussed in Chapter 8. In building an alliance, the five components used with the child are just as vital when trying to achieve a therapeutic alliance with the parent. The aim of this work is to move parents from a state of blocked care and defensiveness to one that allows them to demonstrate more of the qualities of regulation, reflection, and safety with their child. When a therapist uses the DDP model the parents, they will experience regulation, reflection, and safety first-hand, through the provision of those qualities from the therapist. Readers interested in how an attachment formed approach using these components works specifically at the neurobiological level can refer to *The Neurobiology of Attachment-Focused Therapy: Enhancing Connection & Trust in the Treatment of Children & Adolescents* (Baylin & Hughes, 2016).

The following is a generalized example in which some of the five components of the model (follow-lead-follow, affective-reflective dialogue, and PACE) are used to create an experience of relational safety with a parent. This technique helps the therapist deepen the empathy and compassion they have for the parent and, almost simultaneously, the parent's capacity to reflect and feel empathy for their child. It also illustrates how the presence of a safe partner can be harnessed. The parents are Tom (of prime interest here) and Alice, who adopted Brandon, who is now 12 years old. Child-specific blocked care has been identified for Tom. Brandon has an older adopted sister Liz who is 16 years old, and there are no signs of blocked care for Tom and Alice in their relationship with Liz. The family has received DDP with Brandon's involvement. Brandon has a predominately avoidant pattern of relationships, evident in a tendency to turn away from comfort. He holds a negative view of himself and others, which appears to have developed from a background of serious neglect.

THERAPIST: It's been a couple of weeks. . .

TOM: Yes, it has!

THERAPIST: And since then, I've been in touch with Alice. She tells me you really struggled with the resurgence in Brandon's difficulties a few weeks back. That she noticed you were down and irritable . . . hard to reach.

TOM: Yes I did, but I'm over that now.

THERAPIST: That's great to hear, and that Brandon is doing so well again, but I was thinking about how Brandon's difficulties with trust may come back at times, and about how you might feel the next time things became difficult.

TOM: [Unsure] Yes . . . OK.

THERAPIST: Can you tell me more about what happened that made it so hard to reach out when things were so difficult?

TOM: I don't know. I just got down; really down. I couldn't sleep and went into a spiral because this kept happening. I couldn't keep my temper with him. I was getting angry with Brandon or storming off. I thought we were all over that now. It was not good. Not good at all.

THERAPIST: [Empathizes] Oh . . . And so when Brandon's difficulties seemed to come back, it seemed to affect you deeply.

TOM: Yeah. I thought we hadn't achieved much I suppose. But it's all good now.

THERAPIST: Tom, you seem eager to tell me how well things are now. And that you are fine. We've known each other a little while now. It reminds me of how Brandon sometimes shuts you out, as he has learned to be so reliant on himself.

TOM: Yeah in a way it does! Am I in the therapy chair now? [Laughing]

THERAPIST: [Laughs] I guess you may be! Would it be ok to explore that pattern for you? It may not only help us understand you, and what to do next time, but also how Brandon feels when you try to help.

TOM: [Laughs] Yes ok. [Turns to Alice] You know what this is about don't you, love?

ALICE: Yes I do. Shall I say?

TOM: Suppose that would be good. [Eye contact drops, head goes down]

ALICE: Growing up, Tom had an older sister with disabilities. She's lovely but it was tough going for Tom. His parents had their hands full and so . . . [Looks at Tom]

TOM: . . . I just kept things quiet.

THERAPIST: [With acceptance] Kept things to yourself when things were difficult.

TOM: Yes. I didn't want any more stress for my parents, so I just got on with it.

THERAPIST: I'm sorry. That sounds like it was really difficult for you. So when things seem difficult now, and maybe for Alice too, you cope the only way you know.

TOM: Yes . . .

THERAPIST: How hard for you! As you grew up, you learnt quickly how to be with people. Like for all of us, it was the only way you knew. And when things were hard recently, you coped that way. I wonder if you didn't want to upset Alice.

TOM: No I didn't. [Head drops]

THERAPIST: You felt you had to manage how everyone was feeling when you were struggling yourself. [Sighs]

TOM: Yes.

THERAPIST: When Alice told me you were depressed, I was worried for you, too. She seemed to understand what was happening, but she said it was hard to reach you.

ALICE: Yes, it was. He kept saying he was fine, and I was suffering because I didn't know how to help!

THERAPIST: Tom was managing the best he could. You were

managing the best you could. But it was difficult to reach out to one another.

ALICE: Yes. [Looking at therapist] I do love him so.

THERAPIST: [Playfully] That's lovely for me to know but could you tell Tom that?

ALICE: [Laughs, then looks at Tom] I do love you!

TOM: [Tries to downplay the situation, but raises his head, and with some playfulness] Alright! Alright!

THERAPIST: I think your wife is trying to say she loves you because she knows you try and manage everything yourself . . . is that right Alice?

ALICE: Yes. [Getting tearful]

THERAPIST: And life has been hard for you again. Brandon's difficulties have been so worrying. When they got better, I wonder if you thought that was it—problems over!

TOM: Yes, I did.

THERAPIST: But I think Alice is saying you don't need to be alone, but she gets that you try and manage like that, by yourself, like you always had to. Is that right Alice?

ALICE: Yes it is; it can be so hard. I don't want him to feel alone.

THERAPIST: I wonder how this is feeling Tom . . . you have two people trying to reach out to you . . .

TOM: Bit weird!

THERAPIST: It feels different.

TOM: Yes it does.

THERAPIST: I wonder, too, how Brandon feels when you try and get close when he's struggling.

TOM: Like this! [Laughs but uncomfortable]

THERAPIST: That's it! I thought that too.

TOM: I guess I feel bad about taking up time and maybe you don't feel I'm dealing with it very well . . .

THERAPIST: I wonder if you feel bad about yourself at those times.

TOM: Yes, I feel I have let people down.

THERAPIST: That must be difficult, a difficult place to be.

[Alice hugs Tom, who puts his head down again.]

THERAPIST: I see how much you are trying to be the father you think you should be.

TOM: I just want Brandon to let me in, you know, not shut me out when he's got a problem, you know? [Seems tearful]

THERAPIST: Of course. But you never expected that thinking about your life growing up might come up in parenting Brandon. This is hard.

TOM: No, I didn't! [Playfully points to his chair] Can I get off the therapy chair now?

THERAPIST: [Laughs]. It was so easy with Liz [Brandon's older adopted sister] wasn't it?

TOM: Totally different. Totally different.

THERAPIST: So, I wonder how knowing this is useful?

TOM: Well, I guess it means it is something about Brandon and how he copes; which is the same as me.

THERAPIST: Yes, I wonder about that.

TOM: And he must feel bad when things are going wrong but can't tell us.

THERAPIST: Yes. [Moderate emphasis]

TOM: Poor kid.

THERAPIST: Yes, poor you and poor Brandon; but staying with you now, I'm sorry you had to manage so much by yourself when you were growing up.

TOM: It left me feeling I wasn't doing very well. And I can see how Brandon is feeling, too. I can't change him just like that. [Clicks fingers]

THERAPIST: I wonder how you are feeling . . .

TOM: Sad. Sad for him and a bit for me, to be honest.

THERAPIST: Yes, it is sad. I'm feeling sad for you too . . . you are both sometimes feeling the same and seeing the world in a similar way. [Pauses] Alice?

ALICE: [Speaking to the therapist] I do love him. [She looks at Tom]

TOM: I love you, too.

THERAPIST: Please feel free to cuddle. [They cuddle and there is a pause to let them recover naturally] So, I wonder if this makes sense now? That being a father, to Brandon especially, has brought up old ways of managing life, which might mean you go it alone but may end up leaving you feeling bad.

TOM: Yes, I need to not feel so bad. I need to tell Alice.

ALICE: Yes. [Softly] Please.

THERAPIST: And this is a start, too, to helping Brandon when things get difficult again.

TOM: And he had it worse, too. Oh my, what must he be feeling? Poor kid.

THERAPIST: I guess you are coming to know that.

TOM: Yes, and maybe I need to stop pushing and just accept he's doing the best he can.

THERAPIST: . . . that you're doing the best you can.

ALICE: Yes, I think I try to help by getting on Tom to change things.

TOM: [Winks at therapist]

ALICE: [Playfully] Stop it Tom, you know I do that! I'm a fixer! Yes, so maybe I need to put the tools down and stop fixing.

THERAPIST: Can you tell Tom that?

ALICE: I'm sorry I try and fix it, it's my way. I know you are trying, but in pain.

TOM: I know, love. I know.

THERAPIST: Tom, I wonder how that feels to know that.

TOM: I don't feel quite so stupid, or bad I guess.

THERAPIST: Alice gets it. And gets you. And I wonder how it will feel when things are hard for Brandon again.

TOM: Different!

ALICE: Yes, I need to remember that.

THERAPIST: I think you may feel that, too, now.

TOM: I do. Yes, I do.

THERAPIST: And Brandon may, too, perhaps even more, the next time he is struggling.

Exploring some of the origins of Tom's specific blocked care with some of the five components raises his own attachment history, and we can move to a place of greater safety, regulation, and reflection. In turn, this moves him into a position where he can read the needs of his son more clearly and feel for his son, too. He may also come to know better his own contribution to the relationship when they become mutually defensive. This offers him the opportunity to see a three-dimensional view of his son which reflects the mistrust he developed due to neglect. In this example, we also can see the importance of harnessing the role of a partner who can offer safety through acceptance and empathy. Often, work with parents involves both participants. The clinician may determine that individual time with each parent is needed when there is a lack of safety between the parents, such as disagreeing with the other's parenting approach or being closed and defensive toward the other's motivations. Hopefully these separate sessions will lead to joint sessions once both parents are able to be a bit open and vulnerable with the therapist and then risk being the same way with their partner.

SIGNS THAT THE PARENT IS READY FOR THERAPY WITH THE CHILD PRESENT

When is a parent ready to work with the child present? If we are to have confidence that there is a home for the child's attachment system that has the requisite warmth, reflectivity, and regulation, we need to consider what, in sessions with parents, would indicate such progress. When a therapeutic alliance is well-established, we may see the following as positive indicators both of the therapeutic alliance and of a sufficient likelihood that work while the child is present is possible:

BLOCKED CARE DECREASES

This would be the most coherent indication that the parent is in a place to offer trust, reflection, and regulation in the presence of their child. We may find that parents describe moments in the intervening time between parent sessions that suggest their parenting systems are less compromised. They may report feeling less stressed. They may describe enjoying time with their child. They may give examples of times they have mentalized the needs of their child. They may describe staying closer to the difficulties the child is experiencing and for longer periods. We may also see some resolution in their sense of themselves as parents, perhaps through insight into their difficulties and their origins. The absence of blocked care, however, is not a necessary precondition, but signs that the strain in each of these systems is decreasing may indicate that with the active involvement of the therapist, the parent will be able to move into interactions with their child that are trust-building, regulated, and reflective. There may be other signs that convey a meaningful reduction in blocked care.

PARENTS REPORT TRYING TO APPLY THE PRINCIPLES OF PARENTING WE HAVE DISCUSSED WITH THEM

The application of these principles may be easier in the comfort and safety of the clinic; applying them in the moment is likely to be more challenging. However, parents who are actively moving toward a relational approach to their child convey the intention to establish safety with them. We may also find that they abandon approaches that may have helped them achieve some sense of safety at the height of the difficulties, such as sanctions, but which they now see were not helpful to building the relationship with their child.

PARENTS CAN "PACE" THEMSELVES

Parents who can bring some of the qualities of PACE to their situation may be moving in a positive direction. These parents demonstrate that they can: be playful and lighter about their contribution to the challenges; accept the feelings that are behind their behaviors ("I know I was trying to teach him something important, but I went about it all wrong"); bring some curiosity to their experience and behaviors ("I wonder why I did that?"); and give themselves some empathy ("I actually felt I was doing the best I could, and I have been trying so hard!").

PARENTS CAN MENTALIZE THEMSELVES AND THEIR CHILD, SHOWING THAT REFLECTIVE FUNCTIONING HAS IMPROVED

Parents who can see their role in the relationship with their child, convey how the child may see them, and reflect on what has influenced them and their behavior are probably moving into a position of safety with their child.

EMOTIONAL REGULATION IMPROVES

Parents who can move into attachment states of mind and affect that reflect more sadness and regret rather than shame and defensiveness may be moving toward being ready for therapy with their child. We may see this in our interactions with them and in the way they describe situations and examples with their child at home.

PARENTS TOLERATE THE THERAPIST'S LEAD WHEN THEY SAY SOMETHING THAT MIGHT UNDERMINE THEIR CHILD'S SENSE OF SAFETY

An example might be:

> **THERAPIST:** John, I worry that the way you addressed that might cause your son to feel that you are disappointed in him, not simply frustrated with his choice, but disappointed in him. If you agree, would you mind saying it this way instead, if this reflects what you think and feel?

If such suggestions strain the therapeutic alliance, the parent also needs to be willing to engage in relationship repair with the therapist.

PARENTS ARE OPEN TO EXPLORATION

If there is some aspect that may be understood differently from your point of view and the parent is open to this alternate perspective, this suggests a degree of safety. If the parent has some initial defensiveness in response to your point of view or your suggestion, and yet with some repair to the relationship, whatever its conclusion (you may be wrong of course!), they resume the open and engaged state with you, then this also may be a positive sign.

Jamie was referred to therapy for behavioral problems. Here is an example of a session with Adam, Jamie's father, who is beginning to demonstrate that he is moving into a place of safety, reflection, and regulation, which suggests that directly involving Jamie in therapy may now be possible:

THERAPIST: Adam, I have some questions that came up. Do you mind if I cover these?

ADAM: OK.

THERAPIST: Sooo, I was wondering about your time growing up. What . . . er . . . what did you . . . how did your parents respond to you when you were worried or anxious?

ADAM: When I was a kid?

THERAPIST: Yes, if you can.

ADAM: Phew! Been a long time since I thought about that one. Errr. A kid . . . errrr . . .

THERAPIST: Mmm, I wonder if my question was a bit up front. I also fumbled the paper to find my questions, so I wonder if that made a difference?

ADAM: Did you? No worries. I don't think about that time much.

THERAPIST: I wonder why?

ADAM: It doesn't come up. I don't go there too much.

THERAPIST: Yes and I've challenged that just that by asking you about it. I'm sorry if this is a challenge.

ADAM: No worries. My parents were hardworking, and we didn't have much. They gave us a good childhood, they stuck it out when many didn't, and I know that they loved my brother and me. So, yeah. We didn't have money worries or rather we didn't have to worry about that.

THERAPIST: Thanks, and when you were worried, I wonder what happened then?

ADAM: Well. . . That was something I don't remember. I don't think they had the time.

THERAPIST: I see, so they had to work hard to save you and your brother worrying about money but that meant there was less time for you.

ADAM: I didn't feel left out.

THERAPIST: It makes me think about what you did when you had a worry. . .

ADAM: I got on with it!

THERAPIST: No need for anything else! All by yourself! When Jamie has a worry, what does that feel like for you?

ADAM: He doesn't say much so I will leave him sometimes, let him burn it off in his room kinda thing. But he then starts busting out and that's the firecracker moment.

THERAPIST: I wonder . . . is it hard to know what to do? He doesn't say he needs you and maybe you are not sure what to do because you had parents who had to let you get on with things yourself.

ADAM: I did.

THERAPIST: So you can feel for him, but he doesn't come to you and you're not sure whether to go to him. Oh . . . Adam that kinda makes me feel sad for you both. Like you are different places but feeling the same things.

ADAM: I guess I am. I mean I guess we do. I didn't think that before; we both don't know what we are doing! Oh man. Oh I wish I could tell him right now.

THERAPIST: I wonder what you would tell him?

ADAM: That I had no idea how he felt at the time, but I feel the same thing. I missed out and I don't want him to miss out too. Miss out on having someone around.

THERAPIST: I think telling him that could be about the best idea. Adam you really are trying to figure this out. I'm impressed you are looking back, too. To find some answers.

All of these features are not fool-proof assurances that the parent is now ready to maintain these qualities in therapy with the child. Nor can the therapist assume they will need to focus their attention only on the child in parent and child sessions. Parents, with chronic blocked care in particular, may need more time and more help to get to a place of safety and trust. However, if safety is acquired, they can demonstrate that the window for tolerance and safety has been increased and is felt with the therapist. Safety can, like a secure attachment relationship, be returned to at points of need, such as stressful times, and gives the best chance that qualities of regulation and reflection will be directed toward their child.

In the next three chapters, we discuss how the five components are used in DDP to develop the triad of trust, emotional regulation, and reflective functioning with children and families.

chapter five

Developing Trust: Engaging In Reciprocal Conversations

In this book, we highlight the role of attachment in three major areas of development: relationships built on trust, emotional regulation, and social cognition, including reflective functioning. We now focus on a central aspect of secure relationships, namely, the readiness and ability to engage in reciprocal conversations, which, beyond the parent meeting the infant's core biological needs for safety, are at the core of what builds trust and launches the child on their developmental pathway. Within the trust inherent in these reciprocal conversations, the infant becomes primed for developing their emotional regulation and reflective functioning—abilities that will be explored in the next two chapters.

Our first conversations occur in our nonverbal communications that we have with our parents or caregivers when we are infants. We are joined in synchronized movements of vocal and facial expressions along with bodily gestures and posture. These have become known as "call and response" or "serve and return" cycles, in which there is a flowing rhythm between the initiatives and responses of the infant and adult. Through the synchronization of these movements, meaning is cocreated within and between the minds of each. During these conversations, the infant is developing a sense of self, organized around the infant's emerging awareness of her parent's experience of her (e.g., delightful, interesting, clever, lovable). The infant is discovering that she—and her unique qualities—exists in the mind of her parent as her parent exists in her mind. They are so synchronized that, one might say, when things are going well, the infant and parent are functioning together as one in their joint experience of the world and of each other.

These conversations most certainly function best when the infant feels safe within the relationship. When she sees her parent's experience of love and interest and enjoyment, she wants to continue the conversation and have more of them. When she is in distress and experiences her parent's comfort, she will also want to continue. In experiencing joint delight and interest as well as comfort and support, her varying emotional states are being coregulated by the active serve-and-return affective presence of her parents. Over time, the countless conversations that she has with her parents will enable her to develop the ability to autoregulate these emotional states.

In a similar manner, safe conversations enable the infant and young child to develop their social cognition. As she synchronizes her attention and interest with the mind of her parent, she is discovering her parent's perspective, which is often different from her own. She is learning to read the mind of her parent, just as she is discovering her own mind as her parent responds to it and helps her to identify the similarities and differences between their two minds. She is now able to rely on others to deepen and make more comprehensive her own social cognitions. She discovers the value of sharing her inner life with her parent as well as the importance of cooperation in attaining a mutual goal.

When she experiences her parents as being angry with her or indifferent to her, she does not feel safe, and she withdraws from these conversations. She does not want to perceive her parent's mind if it has a negative response to her. Similarly, she does not want to initiate sharing her mind with her parent if she anticipates that her parent will respond negatively. The more that she does not feel safe with her parents, the fewer times she will engage in a conversation with them. Without ongoing safety with her parents, she is not likely to develop the skills needed to be able to engage in conversations in a way that will lead to both emotional regulation and social cognition. With safety, conversations are easy; without safety, they become very difficult.

A child who does feel safe with her parents will still have difficulties engaging in conversations during the routine experiences of socialization when her parent is evaluating her behaviors and placing limits on them. These early differences in perspective about the value of the child's behavior are likely to create some anxiety, leading to protest or withdrawal. A sensitive parent notes the difficulty that her child has with these limits, supports the child through the associated distress, and repairs the relationship sufficiently so that the child again enters into a conversation. With repetition, the child realizes that she is still safe with her parent. The parent continues to love and accept the child even if she does not accept the behavior. In fact, the relationship may well be enhanced when the child begins to trust that the parent is setting the limit—a limit that may well frustrate the child—because learning to behave differently is, in fact, in the child's best interest.

When the parent and child disagree too frequently with regard to what is best, when the conflicts become persistent and hard to resolve, there tends to be an avoidance of these trust building conversations between the parent and child. The parent often becomes uninterested in what the child thinks, feels, and wants. The parent just wants the child to do what she is told! The child loses interest in what the parent is thinking and what the parent's intentions are. The child just wants the parent to stop being so bossy! Each is now focusing primarily on the behavior of the other! Their relationship is now in danger of becoming a cycle of lectures and rules on the one side and defiance and resentment on the other. The value of conversations in assisting the child in regulating his emotional states and deepening his social cognition is minimal. Conversations are replaced by irritated words that are simply expressions of each one's efforts to control the behavior of the other.

If mistrust is high, there may be frequent moments in your sessions when the child does not engage well in reciprocal conversations, either with you or with his parents. Sharing interests, experiences, and perspectives may seem of little value to the child. The child often either refuses to talk or insists on controlling what is being said, limiting the conversation to a few safe topics or changing the topic continuously so that there are few openings to either understand or influence the perspective of the other. This often increases the risk of you being reduced to giving a series of lectures, information, or behavioral recommendations or being content to settle for "small talk" again and again.

When you focus on "the problem" when meeting with the child alone or in a family session, you may find this often makes the problem worse. After a series of defensive claims and counterclaims, the conflicts and differences only seem to be greater. The therapy office may create less safety than is usually present at home because strategies of avoidance might be less effective in the office. Cooperation is not emerging, and instead there is heightened competition to prove who is right and who is wrong.

It is much better for you to focus instead on helping the child—and parents—to feel safe enough during the session that they are able to begin to have conversations with each other—to be truly open and engaged, sharing and understanding the experiences and perspectives of each other about all sorts of things. It is the process—not the problem—that requires the therapist's focus. The problem is a result of a break down in the process. The process involves being willing and able to have conversations with each other. When the problem is blended into the relationship through engagement in varied conversations, the problem becomes just one aspect of an intimate relationship. It is one more thing to have a conversation about—to understand each other's perspective about. When the relationship—and the conversation—is bigger than the problem, a way forward that meets the developmental needs of both the child and the family is likely to emerge. It is within such conversations that mutual trust develops.

There is an everydayness about conversations that tends to cause us to take them for granted. Just as for years many researchers had taken for granted the synchronized nonverbal reciprocity between the parent and infant. We saw those interactions as being cute and fun, and we believed that they helped to make the day-to-day care of an infant more enjoyable. What took much longer to see is how those interactions were crucial not only for the depth and safety of the parent–infant relationship but also for the infant's neurological, physiological, emotional, cognitive, and social development. And still, at times we forget. Little wonder therefore that we underestimate the crucial role of conversations (and playfulness!) in therapy. When the conversation seems forced or dismissive or fragmented, we often simply assume that the therapeutic theme is too difficult to talk about. Yet, it may only be too difficult to talk about because the child—or the adult—may not have the conversational abilities they need to talk about it! This reality might be associated with attachment insecurities as well as difficulties coregulating emotional states and difficulties reflecting on the internal working models of another.

Why do we continue to have conversations long after the developmental processes facilitated by the parent–infant conversations have been mostly attained? What makes them so prevalent in our lives? Let us bring things home for a moment and reflect on what is so enjoyable about having a good conversation with a trustworthy friend. The pleasure we experience is likely due to many factors:

- We feel safe and accepted.
- We feel understood, sensing that our friend "gets it."
- We feel close to our friend as we share ourselves and cooperate in a joint activity.
- We are learning about our friend and the world through discovering our friend's perspective.
- We experience our friend valuing our perspective.
- We are developing a deeper understanding of an object or event than we could have alone.
- We feel more confident in the validity of what we experience when it is shared with and accepted by our friend.

Since these reasons seem to bring great value to our conversations in our everyday lives, it is likely they similarly could greatly enhance the value of therapy, too. The daily conversations within families who seek therapy often do not demonstrate the above features. Within these children and families, their conversations often dwell on problems with anger, frustration, and negative assumptions. They quickly lose the sense of psychological safety necessary for them to occur as they were meant to! Conversations are complex ways of combining the past with the present, reflection with communication, thinking with feeling. Without ongoing safety and trust in one another, they tend to break down and not demonstrate their integrative and meaning-making functions. When that occurs, what we have called a conversation is now nothing more than giving a lecture or information, telling someone why they are right or wrong and what they need to do—a vehicle for angry words!

In light of the above, we hope that the goal of understanding and resolving "the problem" will be set quite a ways into the future. We first need to establish sufficient safety, from which we can develop synchronized, reciprocal conversations, which in turn creates trust, which further enhances the ability for the conversation to explore new meanings of self and others, including discovering strengths and vulnerabilities. When the problem becomes reflected upon in this context, it is not a threat to the relationship, nor does it create shame about the self.

IDEAS FOR BUILDING AND MAINTAINING THERAPEUTIC CONVERSATIONS

ESTABLISH AND MAINTAIN RELATIONAL SAFETY

The conversation will be of short duration if we therapists are not able to establish and maintain the child (and parent's) sense of safety from beginning to end. Safety begins and ends with us. The therapist focuses on maintaining the open and engaged attitude that is described so well by Stephen Porges in his polyvagal theory. To be open and engaged, we need to be able to accept the child regardless of what the child is saying or doing. Even when the therapist needs to place a limit on the child's behavior (trying to throw something through the window!), we still need to strive to accept the thoughts, feelings, and wishes that led to that behavior. When we are open and engaged, the child will tend to become open and engaged—not defensive— as well. If the child does become defensive, and we are able to remain open and engaged, the child's defensiveness is likely to become weaker and of shorter duration. This open and engaged attitude is communicated to the child primarily nonverbally, which we will now explore.

BE AWARE OF THE RANGE OF
BEING OPEN AND ENGAGED

Chapter 1 described how the polyvagal theory predicts that safety in relationships (conveyed by nuanced nonverbal signals from one person to the other) activates the social engagement system in the autonomic nervous system and that this system enables us to be open to and engaged with others in our environment. When we are not experiencing safety, we become defensive, with our attention being directed primarily toward identifying aspects of our environment that are a threat to us and choosing ways of interacting with the environment that we think will be most likely to regain our safety (fight, flight, freeze with vigilance). These responses are so instantaneous that we react without being aware of making a choice to defend ourselves.

We now explore the range of experiences within the social engagement system that are available to us when we are safe. Most often we speak of being open and engaged while relating with others when we are feeling safe. We are open to being influenced by the other and learning from the other while at the same time being engaged with the other in a reciprocal manner. As the other is communicating with us, we are responding, and our response influences the other, guiding their further initiatives with us. The safety and engagement are created between us.

When we are in a new situation, or attempting to experience an old situation from a new perspective, being open and engaged gives us the safety and mental state we need to best explore, discover, and understand what we are attending to. The goal of therapy is not to change past situations but to change the experience of those situations. A past event may have become associated with fear and shame, discouragement and resignation. Through being open and engaged with a therapist's curious explorations, the child (and parents) may now experience that past event with new meaning, hope, and confidence, without shame or fear. This is the cutting edge of therapy. Our skill as a therapist involves generating sufficient safety and confidence so that the child will follow or walk alongside us into those past events in order to cocreate new meanings.

There is another aspect of the social engagement system, in which the tone of engagement is more about connection than exploration. This is the relaxed and connected state. Being relaxed and connected simply involves being engaged with each other in the day-to-day. It is light conversations, being playful, sharing daily experiences, joining in shared activities, cooperating, and planning future activities. These day-to-day, enjoyable, shared activities provide a backdrop of safety and connection in which trust and belonging develop. In the background, there is a sense of comfort, mutual acceptance, light discovery as we share some laughter and experiences together. In therapy, much of the time will be spent getting to know each other in this relaxed connected state. This is the foundation from which the more active, deep exploration of open and engaged states can happen. The phrase *relaxed and connected* was developed by Deborah Page, a psychologist in Brighton, England (personal communication), to describe the experience of something important going on that is essential to the therapeutic process but is less dramatic than the open and engaged moments of deeper exploration.

There is a third aspect of the social engagement system that does not involve as much outward-looking exploration as the open and engaged state, nor the light companionship of the relaxed and connected state. This third state is when we are *safely still* in the presence of those with whom we are safe. We may simply be sitting together quietly with a strong thread of connection and comfort running between us. Trauma erodes the ability to be safely still, filling up the quiet spaces with terror and shame. In therapy, when we are able to support our clients to feel safe enough to be still, we help them to be in parts of their minds that previously terrified them and from which they have run away. This state allows reflection and new meaning-making; our presence helps the client to feel safe enough that they don't need to run away from the contents of their mind that had previously held them hostage. Safe stillness facilitates reflection, which then facilitates integration of the new meanings that were cocreated in the open-engaged state. The phrase *safely still* was first used by Deb Dana (2018) while describing the application of the polyvagal theory to therapy. Dana created this phrase when speaking of the neurobiological state described by Stephen Porges as *being immobilized without fear.*

We believe that there is value in therapy in considering social engagement as a continuum from open-and-engaged to relaxed-and-connected to safely-still. You may find that the explorations of being open and engaged and safely still are likely to create some anxiety in the therapy session that will reduce the client's sense of safety and cause a child or parent to withdraw from the therapeutic conversation about the stressful event. At these moments, we need to reconnect and rediscover the relaxed connected state before new exploration and integration can occur. You might be wise to begin each session developing the relaxed and connected interactions with the client. This will lead to lighter, reciprocal conversations that will deepen the sense of safety and create the client's experience of being connected with you. The momentum of this safe conversation is likely to enable the client to move with you into the explorative state of being open and engaged. In this state, you will be cocreating a new story of past events. Later in the session, you might transition back to being relaxed and connected, and then when you reflect during the course of the session or at the end of the session, the client is likely to transition with you into the safely still quiet state that enables reflection and integration of the meanings that you are cocreating together.

BE AWARE OF AND ATTEND TO OUR NONVERBAL COMMUNICATIONS

Nonverbal bodily communications generate safety and trusting relationships when they express relational experiences of acceptance, interest and delight, warmth and care, fascination and commitment. These communications are conversations because they involve the minds of both individuals. If we are to bring the findings of attachment into our therapeutic relationships, we need to communicate these experiences and communicate them clearly. A more traditional "neutral stance," in which we are ambiguous in our communications of our experience of the child, is likely to generate anxiety and doubt and is not likely to create a secure, attachment-based relationship. When we convey safety, the other is likely to feel safe. When we convey defensiveness, the other is likely to become defensive. When we are ambiguous, the other is likely to "play it safe" and become defensive.

VOICE PROSODY

Our voice can affect our attention, mood, and engagement, much like a musical instrument does. In having a conversation with a child—or adult—how we say things is often more important than what we say. The impact of saying to a child "You did your best" varies greatly, depending on whether there was a note of disappointment, indifference, encouragement, or pride in your voice.

Voice prosody, defined as the nonverbal aspects of our speech that convey attitude and emotions, include many factors that greatly influence the nature of the conversation.

1. Rhythm and cadence may create (or threaten) an experience of acceptance and safety that may be carried into the felt meaning of the words being expressed.
2. Varying intensity and beat may hold the child's interest and create a positive anticipation for what is coming next.
3. Brief periods of silence, pausing, whispering, sudden outbursts of excitement also hold the child's interest and create a positive expectation.

> **THERAPIST:** I wonder, John. [Pause] It bothered you a lot, really a lot . . . when your mom did not scold your little sister. [Pause] Does it seem . . . does it seem that sometimes your little sister is more special to your mom than you are?

> **JOHN:** [Reflecting] Not more special . . . just better than me.

4. Expressions of uncertainty/suspense leading to surprise keeps the child's mind open (and engages the prefrontal cortex) to what he is discovering moment to moment in the conversation.
5. Heightened animation generates regulated confidence, whereas agitation generates dysregulated apprehension.
6. Repetition of words, phrases, or movements tend to highlight and intensify the experience that is being conveyed in the conversation.

> **THERAPIST:** Wait! Wait! Wait! I think that's it! [Pause while looking out the window] Of course you're angry

with me! You had told me a few minutes ago that it seems that no one ever listens to you! [Shorter pause] And now! And now! I just asked you the same question that I asked you before—like I didn't hear what you told me . . . like I didn't hear . . .

CHILD: So why should I bother telling you anything! You don't listen either.

THERAPIST: [Much softer and slower] And I don't listen either . . . I'm your therapist . . . your therapist! And sometimes I . . . don't . . . I don't listen either.

FACIAL EXPRESSIONS

Facial expressions, too, enable the child or adult to experience the therapist's emotional tone and intensity of interest and motivation.

1. Curious eyes or puzzled looks hold the child's interest and increase their receptivity to what is coming next.
2. A gradually emerging smile or more rapid movement of arms and hands conveys a sense of increasing animation of a positive experience or confidence in what is happening next.
3. Covering your face with your hands while repeating a word or phrase leaves the child with heightened anticipation of what is coming next. It tends to emphasize your deliberation . . . your concentration on the theme . . . how important it is to you to understand it, to get it right.
4. Facial expressions often work in unison with voice prosody to amplify the effect of achieving greater interest, safety, curiosity, and confidence. (When you are silent while your

face shows an increasing sense of understanding and excitement, the child is most often fully open, engaged, and confident in what he is about to learn. The silence is highlighting your facial expressions to increase their impact.)

5. The therapist can convey a sense of urgency to understand and be helpful by increasing the intensity and beat of his voice and making a facial expression that conveys an intense focus on the specific content of the conversation. At other times, the therapist's facial expressions may convey a relaxed, wide-angle perspective, a sense of drifting with wherever the conversation leads. The contrast between these two facial expressions alerts the client to the perceived importance of the content conveyed with this sense of urgency.

THE NONVERBAL MEANINGS OF THE STORYTELLER

The rhythmic and varied tones and intensities along with dramatic facial expressions are common while storytelling, just as they are during parent–infant conversations. The storyteller holds the interest of the other person by varying the facial and vocal expressions so that they convey suspense, uncertainty, interest, surprise, and excitement, along with the actual words being expressed. These communications have a flow to them that generate a sense of safety because they are simply describing and understanding events and experiences without evaluating them. When communications lack a nonverbal rhythm and flow they tend to become monotone, uninteresting, while also being experienced as lectures in which the speaker is telling the listener what is right or wrong, what needs to be done or not, and whether the child should feel shame or pride over his behavior. Within the lecture or information giving, there is little or no conveyed interest in the experience of the other. It is not reciprocal.

The storytelling voice and facial expressions ensure that the focus of the conversation is not restricted to behavior and its evaluation nor only to the mind of one person. The focus instead is on the various meanings of the event, the context in which it occurred, and how it was experienced by each. This way of communicating in therapy ensures that the intent is to understand, not judge. If we use a monotone expression the child experiences an evaluation and immediately becomes defensive. Even if the evaluation is positive, the child assumes a self-protective stance, being vigilant about the evaluations yet to come. Evaluations give, and evaluations take.

A story telling tone in therapy is still a conversation, even if you are taking most of the lead in the telling. The child's active listening is also contributing to the story. While the words might be predominately yours, the nonverbal expressions tend to be reciprocal. In this way, the story being developed is cocreated. As you are speaking in developing the story, you are noting the child's nonverbal responses, and these greatly influence your subsequent emphases and directions of the story.

The events and experiences of the child's life tend to be the primary content that are developed into stories. Facts are present, but the focus is more on the experience of the facts and their meanings in the child's narrative. There is a beginning, middle, and end. When the child's behavior ("the problem") is the central focus of the story, the behavior is given a context in which it occurs. Its meaning is often understood as a natural, understandable result of the context. Normalizing the behavior within the context tends to reduce any associated shame.

As she was exploring an event in which a boy swore at his father, the therapist suddenly became animated and exclaimed,

"NOW I THINK THAT I UNDERSTAND! You thought that your dad was disappointed in you! You even thought that he wished that he had another son! Now I can see why you became so angry with him!" The event is the same, but now the boy—and his father—understand the meaning of the event in a way that enabled both to address the recent strain on their relationship without defensiveness and shame.

The story plot that emerges tends to be multifaceted. It may be interesting, amusing, inspiring, informative, and surprising while also scary, sad, upsetting, and irritating. As the story is cocreated by you, child, and parent, it tends to move toward coherence. The events within the story tend to make sense, given the other aspects of the story. As they make sense, sometimes guilt and remorse emerge over certain actions of the child, but shame seldom arises. When the child is engaged in the cocreation of the story with new meanings of his behavior, he is often able to do so without defensiveness.

As the story is developing, either you, the child, or the parent is likely to go off on a tangent. This is not surprising, as it often happens in most conversations that we have with friends and family. There tends to be a meandering quality to good conversations, often allowing space to the interests and ideas of each person. Holding strongly to one theme may undermine the sense of safety and joint activity that is needed for the conversation to emerge. Being narrowly focused on one theme may seem too much like a lecture rather than a conversation.

The tangents may introduce partially related events, or they may serve to provide a bit of relief to the intensity of the developing primary story. There is value in accepting the tangent and going along with it a bit. Go with the child into what he introduced, but do not forget to finish the original story! You can do this easily: "That's interesting, Johnny, how your friend learned to do that, thanks for telling me . . . now, what were we talking about before you thought of your friend?" And this might happen more than once. If this process is accepted, it is not a power struggle! It's a conversation!

Because holding onto the thread of the story as the conversation flows may be quite hard for the child, you need to be skilled at not forgetting the central theme while going off on a tangent or two. You also need to keep in mind that a number of tangents may suggest that the child experiences the core theme as too anxiety provoking, in which case you need to focus on the child's safety before going further with the story. You might do so by reflecting on it a bit, conveying empathy for the difficulty, setting aside part of it, or setting aside further exploration until the child is more ready to explore it further.

Other times, the child may be focused on one tangent quite strongly. It is possible that it is a related theme that has more meaning for the child at that moment. He may have a greater sense of urgency to understand this tangent than he does the original theme. In this case, it is likely best to follow the child's lead and explore this new theme, setting aside the original one for another day.

> Sue, a nine-year-old adopted girl, had never spoken with her adoptive parents or her previous therapist about her life before being adopted when she was five. With the story telling voice, and while wondering about her relationships with her adoptive parents, the therapist casually asked why her adoptive parents chose her. Sue replied easily that she thought it was because she was pretty, and she went on to say that her last foster mother, Rita, had thought that she was pretty too. After a bit of talking about her foster home the therapist wondered if her biological parents also had thought that she was pretty. Sue said they did not, and she

went on to say that they were the mean parents. After chatting a bit about her biological parents, the girl spontaneously returned to talk about Rita. The therapist redirected the child back to her biological parents. Again, the child engaged a bit about her life with her biological parents and then returned to speak about her foster mother. The therapist decided that, right now, this was the most important part of Sue's story about her life-before-adoption, and so they became fully engaged about memories of her time in her foster home. Soon she began to cry about missing Rita. As this part of her story deepened, she paused and said sadly that she was a bad girl and that's why her foster mother did not keep her. With comfort from her adoptive parents, she then grieved the loss of her foster mother, something she had never done outwardly in her four years of adoption. In the next session, her mind easily moved into her life before being adopted. This time she did want to speak more about her "mean" parents and wondered why they were mean to her. As she explored this, she realized that this was when she first thought that she was bad. She remembered that she had stopped thinking she was bad when in foster care, until she had to leave and she began thinking that again. As the conversation continued its journey, her focus flowed naturally to her adoptive parents, and she wondered if they ever thought that she was bad when she misbehaved. Within the context of their comfort and empathy for her, she was able to cry again, seemingly while releasing a pervasive sense of shame that she had carried since birth.

Why are we having this conversation? Not to fix the problem. Not to fix the child either, though children do tend to develop in comprehensive ways through such conversations. They tend to be more ready to trust, their emotions tend to be more regulated, and they are likely to engage more easily in reflecting about their internal working models. The purpose of the developing story is to get to know the child better and to help the child to get to know himself better. Many children who struggle with shame or who have not developed the habit of reflecting on their inner lives tend not to know themselves in a way that involves having developed a coherent life story. Having a conversation with an adult with whom the child feels safe is likely to facilitate their ability to do so. "Fixing the problem" often results from these developing conversations, but it is not the goal for having them. If it were the goal, the child would quickly retreat to defensiveness, since your intention would nonverbally convey your stance as evaluative, not accepting.

Yes, your primary intention as therapist in a relationship centered therapy is to get to know all aspects of the child. You are likely to begin with those features that the child invites you to know. From there you get to know aspects of the child and her life that naturally emerge within your conversations. As you know more and more about the child, you will become aware of gaps in the child's history, and you can casually inquire about them, assuming that the child feels comfortable filling in the gaps. At the first sign that the child is not comfortable with these new explorations, you may set aside this new theme for a time in order to maintain the child's sense of safety.

Once there are fewer gaps, you are ready to introduce the "problems" for which the parents or teachers previously expressed concern. The conversation does not change, the flow of your voice and the natural expressions of playfulness (when called for), acceptance, curiosity, and empathy remain part of the conversation just as they were for every other topic that was discussed. The flowing conversation now holds the problem in a way that safely removes the shame or fears associated with it and often enables the child to speak about it much more fully and easily than before. Now, it is simply part of her story, an important part, yes, as are the parts that might be considered strengths, dreams, habits, worries, and moments of joy and laughter and doubt.

While you get to know the child—the whole child—you consistently convey a habitual attitude of acceptance and enjoyment. You show that you enjoy spending time with the child. Your focus is the child and her life—all of her life. The problem has a place in her life, but it is not her. She is not first a diagnosis, a symptom, a victim, or a survivor. She is a child, and you enjoy being with her as you get to know her.

The story has rhythm of its own. You ensure that the momentum, the flow, glides from one theme to another. Whether the themes be easy or hard, the story continues. You do not stop and get serious when the theme addresses "the problem." That serious tone suggests work, may trigger a "this is hard" attitude, and will likely create defensiveness. It is the continuing flow of your voice that keeps the explorations safe. The conversational story can often hold the most stressful theme and dissipate the anxiety or shame that emerges. The prosody of your voice and the openness of your face produce much safety and have the power to reduce the fear or shame associated with whatever the content is.

STAYING IN SYNC

Children who have difficulty relating in a reciprocal, synchronized manner present challenges for therapists. It is much easier to be safely engaged with children who initiate and respond in interactions, much like how a healthy infant or young child does. When a child does not do so, it is important to not assume that they do not want to or that they are "resistant." A more accurate assumption would be that having a reciprocal conversation is difficult, awkward, or confusing for them. Their defensive response may be their only choice. The following sections represent various scripts that represent times when the child is facing conversational challenges that seem difficult to him for various reasons. Our responses are designed to develop our understanding of the child's context and difficulties.

ANGRY

> **CHILD:** Leave me alone! I don't want to talk. I have nothing to say to you!
>
> **THERAPIST:** [Matching the intensity of the child's voice, without being angry in return] I get what you're saying! You're really clear! Would you help me to understand why you don't want to talk with me? [therapist's voice is gradually deceasing in intensity] Wait! Of course, you would not want to! You've already talked with two other therapists, and my guess is that each time it seemed to you that all they wanted to do was find something wrong with you. You don't want that to happen again! [Therapist pauses and looks out the window, giving the child a chance to speak.]

When the child remains silent, the therapist continues:

> **THERAPIST:** Ah! I wonder if you figure that all I'm going to do is tell you not to argue with your teacher/parent and do what you're told. If you think that, of course you don't want to say anything to me. It seems like all I want to do is keep your teacher/parent happy.
>
> **THERAPIST:** [Therapist senses the child wants to argue a bit, not being sure if he wants to become engaged or not, and might respond to a bit of playfulness] Tell you what . . . how about if we

text for five minutes! But I can't say much when I text—I'm pretty slow, so can we compromise and alternate texting and talking?

Or, while looking out the window talking to himself, the therapist says:

THERAPIST: John doesn't want to talk with me. That makes it hard, what can a therapist do if he can't talk? Maybe send signals of some sort. Write notes? If we don't have a conversation about something . . . we both might get pretty bored and nod off.

DISTRACTING

CHILD: Where did you get that picture above your desk? [A minute later] When are we done? [A minute later] I'd like to live in China. [A minute later] When I'm 15, I'm going to be a dancer on TV.

When the therapist responds to one statement or question, the child ignores the response and says something unrelated. After a bit of this the therapist says:

THERAPIST: [With animation, conveying confusion and a bit of light frustration] Wait a second. I was telling you where I got this incredible picture of the ocean and you didn't let me finish! Ok, I do want to know why you want to live in China but how about I tell you about my picture first! Wait a second again! You have not even told me why you want to live in China, you have not let me tell you when we're done and you don't know anything about my picture and now you're telling me about how you want to be a famous dancer! But I'm afraid when I ask about that you'll say something else! We're not going to have a conversation about anything and that makes me crazy! Why not pick something and we'll have a conversation about it! Why not? You pick."

Or using less animation, more slowly and quietly, hoping to get the child's attention with the contrast and gently asking for the child to listen by holding his hands up as he speaks:

> **THERAPIST:** You have so . . . many . . . things to talk with me about. So many things. It seems hard to pick one and to just chat with me about that one. I wonder if it seems that people don't listen to you much and you really want people to show that they are interested in everything you're interested in.

WITHDRAWN

For a seemingly sad child who responds mostly with "I don't know" or "I don't think about it," you might say:

> **THERAPIST:** [Conveys empathy with the child's vulnerable state, waits a moment, and if the child does not initiate a response to empathy, follows with a light, gentle curious comment] It seems that things are really hard for you now, John, really . . . hard." [Pause] I wonder, has it been this way long? [Pause] I wonder what is the hardest now, John?

DEFENSIVE

In response to defensiveness:

> **CHILD:** Ok, I'm not perfect! So I need to see a therapist because I like to fool around and people get upset! I'm not the only one who does that stuff!

THERAPIST: [Matches intensity, then leads into a quieter conversation that might reduce the defensiveness and evoke a bit of openness and vulnerability] It seems to you that you have to be what people want you to be . . . and that's to be perfect! Never make one mistake! If that's how it is—no wonder you're annoyed about being here! And I wonder too, if sometimes . . . you might think . . . that your parents are disappointed in you. That you're not the son they want.

THERAPEUTIC CONVERSATIONS AND EMERGING STORIES

When you, as a therapist, use this model of building a safe, attachment-focused relationship, the child will begin to discover, during the first hour that you spend together, what is likely to be the journey of therapy. You and she will have conversations about many things, many of which she is interested in and will probably enjoy talking about. Other conversations will be about harder things, things that she is likely to avoid talking about—or even thinking about. But again, as you accept her response to these conversations that you initiate and you come to understand, without judgment, why she responds the way she does, she is likely to experience a degree of safety sufficient to explore most themes. Your relaxed and conversational tone will create the experience of safety. She will gradually discover that as she has these conversations, she does not experience the fear or shame that she anticipated. Your nonverbal moment-to-moment expressions along with your gestures and how you notice, understand, and respond to the nonverbal communications that she makes will all help her feel safe. And within this experience of safety, she will begin to trust you and to experience the value of discovering new meanings and possibilities present in all areas of her life.

The pattern of these synchronized moments between you and the child begin to form stories, coherent and comprehensive stories that enable him to better accept and understand the many challenging events, relationships, and behaviors of his life. It leaves him more open to guidance and the ideas of helpful others as he begins to see their positive intentions for what they are. These emerging stories are likely to contain the understanding and skills that he needs to move confidently into the future. His unique and adaptive qualities are likely to become evident, enabling him to shed the habitual defenses and challenging behaviors he used to communicate through. These stories will not emerge without development of the initial safety level required to generate conversations. They will develop with a sense of continuing safety, kept alive from moment-to-moment through interactive repair whenever the engagement loses its synchronized reciprocity. And along the course of this journey, he will be developing a coherent sense of self that is no longer hampered by pervasive fears and shame.

As therapists, we might consider taking a quite active stance in cocreating these stories. At times, a receptive and reflective stance is sufficient and enables the parent and child the space to explore new possibilities for their conflicts and their relationship. Often however, the stories that they develop have been told time and time again, highlight their differences, hold negative assumptions about each other's motives, and avoid any possibility of vulnerability and seeming to be weak in the face of the other's criticism. We might need to actively join the story, notice and initiate a conversation about aspects of the story that might generate hope while reducing shame. The family may be relying on us to uncover realistic meanings that enhance the family experience while at the same time valuing the individual experiences of each member of the family. We must not passively accept a family story that is on the path to hopelessness and blame. Rather we need to lead the story into conversations that generate realistic hope. This hope is not as likely to be created by offering skills that are outside of the family story as it is by joining the story and noticing hopeful possibilities for change that are embedded in their already joint histories.

ATTACHMENT-BASED RECOMMENDATIONS TO GIVE TO PARENTS REGARDING ENGAGING IN RECIPROCAL CONVERSATIONS

1. Remember that conversations are important. They are central to communicating and discovering love and joy, interest and compassion. They teach us all how to share, take turns, cooperate, and engage in give and take. They give us practice in playfulness, being polite, being assertive, and resolving conflicts.

2. Conversation is defined as *an act of talking in an informal way.* Do not forget the word *informal.* That aspect of a conversation is central to its being a safe activity for your children to share their inner lives with you. When conversation becomes formal, it fairly quickly becomes a lecture or a series of questions and answers. Evaluations and judgments often make an appearance.

3. When you and your children are describing experiences, there is much less chance that you or they will be evaluating who is right and who is wrong. The more you stay with describing what you thought, felt, perceived, and imagined, the more likely you will become engaged in mutual story

telling. You will be sharing your individual stories and developing family stories. Within such sharing, the sense of self is enhanced, as is the sense of family relationships.

4. You might frequently use phrases such as "I thought," "It seemed to me," "I wondered," "From my point of view," so that your children (and you) are more likely to remember that our conversations are primarily about our experiences and not about objective facts. Experiences are not right or wrong. Differences are welcome in conversations. Sharing perspectives enables all of us to develop.

5. Your relationships with your children are enhanced when you have more conversations with them and when you give them fewer lectures.

6. Your children will understand what you mean by the word *respect* when the ideas, desires, and emotions of everyone in the family are equally heard and valued during conversations. Respect is the most alive and valuable when it is reciprocal.

7. You might want to give a high priority to conversations during mealtimes, transitions, check-in times, going for walks, and car rides.

8. You might consider that conversations are more important for your children's social-emotional-cognitive development than solitary time alone or with virtual others on screens.

9. There is an Irish proverb that says, "Within the shelter of each other, the people thrive." You might add, "Within the safety of conversations, your children and your family are nourished."

10. Having enjoyable conversations that build trust and companionship are also instrumental in encouraging our children's emotional regulation and development as well, something that we will consider in the next chapter.

chapter six

Facilitating Emotional Regulation

Having seen in earlier chapters how attachment security facilitates emotional regulation, we now turn to what this looks like. Emotion is the word that we use to describe the various forms of energy that give expression to our lives. Sadness, fear, joy, excitement, anger, shame—all are emotions. They are associated with external events or objects of our attention or with internal events—thoughts, memories, fantasies. If we consider emotion to be the energy, then thought would be the information, and together they constitute our experience (combining with our internal and external sensations). It is hard to imagine emotion without some cognitive aspect, no matter how small, or thoughts without some emotional aspect. In our efforts to understand both emotions and thoughts, we place them in separate chapters in this book. In life, they are interwoven, with the one continuously influencing the other.

The primary feature of an infant's experience appears to be emotion! And it is often breathtaking! Appearing and vanishing in a split second. Engulfing her entire body! Considering the focus and intensity of their emotions (even those peaceful moments appear to be all-consuming to the infant), infants seem to be completely in the here-and-now! Without having to practice mindfulness!

Infants are so quick to demonstrate pleasure or displeasure with us, without giving it any thought! Which is good, since the infant does not have many thoughts to give. Her cortex (the part of her brain where her cognitions will be developing) will rearrange a lot after birth as she senses the world and experiences lots of reciprocal engagement with mom and dad, before taking a more active role in experiencing her world.

Yes, it is those reciprocal engagements that are needed for the integrative development of the cortex—and for facilitating the regulation of the intense, seemingly unpredictable comings and goings of the infant's emotions. Initially, we might actually refer to the infant's emotion, not emotions, since it appears to be a global state of energy that advances and retreats at great speed. Again, it is those reciprocal engagements that cause this global state to become differentiated in specific categories of emotion. Early on, this differentiation may involve two states—pleasure and pain—but gradually these two states develop clear or subtle variations within them. It is within reciprocal engagements that the infant is drawn into joint experiences involving expressions of emotion (affects—which are defined as the nonverbal expression of emotion in the voice, face, body) and thinking (focus of attention) and intentions (cooperation). Within these joint emotional experiences, the infant's emotions become regulated (assuming that the parent's emotions were regulated). Within these joint emotional experiences, the infant's emotions begin to differentiate (assuming that the parent has a variety of emotional experiences while engaged with her infant).

During these synchronized, reciprocal experiences with his parent, the infant's emotional states are being coregulated. The infant's affective expressions of his emotions become synchro-nized with his parent's regulated affective expressions and, over time, become more regulated. They become less likely to sud-denly appear and disappear. They are less likely to overwhelm the infant with their intensity. When this joint activity involv-ing the coregulation of emotional experiences occurs again and again, the infant gradually develops the neurological ability to regulate his emotions when he is alone (refer back to Chapter 2). He is able to self-regulate his emotions. Not always of course. But enough so that the life of this lovely infant with these proud parents, now offers more opportunities for peace and quiet.

When the infant's distress becomes increasingly intense (from hunger, a loud noise, becoming cold) the infant becomes frightened by the intensity, which makes it more intense! This escalation continues until the infant sees the eyes of her parent along with facial and vocal expressions that communicate "You are safe," and the intensity stops rising and feels manageable. The infant becomes regulated as the sense of safety communi-cated by the parent replaces the fear. The same is true for excite-ment! The infant's excitement becomes increasingly intense, to the degree that the infant becomes frightened by its intensity. When the infant's excitement is joined with the welcoming eyes, face, and voice of the parent that say "You are safe," the parent's expression of safety replaces the fear.

In the synchronized interaction between the infant and par-ent, the parent communicates safety in his affective expressions and the infant remains or becomes regulated. It is the safety communicated within synchronized affective expressions that creates the coregulation of the infant's emotions. This sense of safety is greatest when the infant is securely attached to his care-giver. A central feature of attachment is its function as a neuro-biological regulatory system.

When the older child is in distress, she may have the self-regulation skills needed to manage the distress without falling into an intense state of terror, rage, or despair. However, if the distress is too extreme, the child may still need the relationship with her attachment figure in order to stay regulated. If the distress is caused by a break in the relationship with her attachment figure, then she is likely to be at a greater risk of dysregulation, often being unable to rely on her attachment figure for coregulation.

When the older child is at risk for dysregulation, still the greatest gift that we have to offer is likely to be the experience of safety and coregulation of the child's emotion within the synchronized engagement. Yet, some parents assume that the child needs to self-regulate his emotional states and be independent, tough, self-reliant, and disciplined. When parents have not had a secure attachment and one which typifies emotional regulation, they will not be able to respond to the emotional needs of their child. When we forget the value of and need for secure attachments throughout life, we forget the value of comfort and support. We are slow to say "Lean on me," and instead, too often:

1. We may ask for too much self-reliance and independence from children and ask for it when they are far too young. We worry that encouraging or even supporting the child to rely on his parents, with whom he is securely attached, will create a dependent child who will "never grow up." We ignore the great volume of research that demonstrates that the child who is securely attached tends to be able to function quite well as an adult by relying both on herself and trusted others as each situation calls for it. They are also resilient in their response to intense challenges, life events, and traumatic events.

2. We tend to evaluate specific emotions negatively to varying degrees. These emotions include anger, fear, and sadness as well as "too much" excitement or playfulness. We then fail to understand the meaning of the emotion or how it functions as an attempt to manage a difficulty.

3. We provide children with coping skills so that they may rely on themselves when in distress. We teach them to self-talk, to employ anger-management techniques, to engage in competing behaviors, to provide their emotions with an appropriate expression, or when all else fails to use the old (unreliable) "count to ten" suggestion. What we forget is that these skills require the active engagement of our cognition. These skills lie in our cortex—our dorsolateral prefrontal cortex especially. The difficulty here is that this area of the brain is slow to develop for all of us. It is especially slow to develop, and may never develop fully, for those exposed to chronic early stress, and it tends to not work when under acute stress that might cause dysregulation. Skills recommended to stop dysregulation are the same skills that do not develop well when chronically dysregulated. They are not effective when we dysregulate!

4. We may isolate the child out of a belief that if we do not "reinforce" the misbehavior seemingly caused by intense rage, this will "extinguish" the behavior. Many children who are isolated often lack the self-regulation skills needed to manage their emotion, even in the best of times. Other children might have those skills during times of mild distress but lose them whenever the distress becomes more intense. Isolation does not facilitate emotional regulation skills! In the short term the child might "calm down." This is often due to the fact that he is exhausted or that he is learning to be submissive (not the best thing to teach a child who is at risk of becoming a victim). Or, he calms when he thinks of a revenge strategy. With revenge, he will not have lost the power struggle!

EMOTIONAL REGULATION THROUGH THE LENS OF ATTACHMENT

SAFETY

We have mentioned the central importance of safety in the previous chapters, we are mentioning it again now, and we will revisit it a few times more. How could we not stress safety if we are writing a book on attachment and its influence on the mental health of children and families? When we are safe, we are open to ways of relating that facilitates our attachment security, and safety supports our development.

As we have stated before, the safety of both child and parent are enhanced when they are relating with each other from the open and engaged state of mind rather than the defensive state of mind. It is the parent's responsibility, when the child is relating defensively, to inhibit her tendency to react defensively herself and to remain in—or quickly return to—being open and engaged. This will evoke a movement toward being open and engaged within the child.

This is all the more true when our child is in danger of becoming emotionally dysregulated. If we lose our sense of safety, we will be in danger of also becoming dysregulated, which will increase the risk that the child will become dysregulated behaviorally as well as emotionally.

The safety produced by the parent's open and engaged state will also help the child remain regulated because the parent's state communicates confidence that the child's intense emotional experience will not be too much for them as they address it together.

A 16-year-old girl screamed at her parents during a treatment session while we were exploring the intensity of her rage outbursts at home. She yelled, "Don't you get it! When I'm screaming at you, I need you! I need you because I'm terrified inside!"

This girl's ability to communicate her complex, paradoxical emotional states to her parents gradually enabled them to remain with her with compassion and confidence that she truly did need them. She needed them to be emotionally strong and safe if she was to be able to reduce her terror of her intense rage and become regulated.

BE REGULATED YOURSELF

Too often therapists work with parents or teachers on managing a child's intense emotional outbursts without exploring whether or not the adult is regulated during the child's dysregulated state. The importance of this was discussed in Chapter 4, and it will be mentioned again in Chapter 8. Given what we now know about how emotions are communicated, how emotions are regulated, and how the child needs to feel safe to remain or become regulated, failure to consider the adult's emotional state during the conflicts cannot be considered "best practice." When adults state defensively, "He made me mad!" they often do so without adding: "Would you help me to develop the skills so that I am able to inhibit my anger when he is acting in a provocative way?"

So, as therapists we need to offer that assistance even if it is not asked for. The parent or teacher may become defensive at what they experience as the implication that it is their fault that the child acts in such a dysregulated way. To which we need to reply:

I'm sorry that I said that in a way to make you think that I was blaming you. That's not what I mean. What I'm saying

is that I have to help you to learn to inhibit a natural tendency to "give as good as you get" when he acts that way.
When you are centered and regulated yourself, you are in
the best position to create a change in his emotional and
behavioral state.

The following example demonstrates how our own attachment history at times plays a central role in our difficulty staying
regulated when our child is being angry or dysregulated:

The therapist, Alice, had spoken with Sue and Brent without their 12-year-old son, Brandon, on three occasions before
beginning joint sessions with the three of them. She had come
to understand the family history, Brandon's strengths and challenges, and the parents' perception of their relationships with
him. She had instructed the parents about PACE and the nature
of the sessions. She was confident that they would be able to
remain regulated and generate safety for Brandon as she explored
their relationships. However, in the second joint session, Brandon yelled at his father, and Brent threatened and screamed at
his son, expressing qualities that Alice had not thought to be
present. She asked Sue and Brent to schedule another session
with her without Brandon.

Alice first worked to help Brent to feel safe enough with
her and Sue to explore his experience of his son at the time
he exploded. After a fairly long discussion, in which he gradually went more deeply into his own attachment history than
he had at the onset of the treatment, Brent was able to say how
overwhelmed he often felt during the frequent times when his
father would scream at him. He spoke of his terror, his shame,
and then his rage at his father over the years. Now they are civil
with each other, but they never sit and have conversations of any
meaning to either of them. Toward the end of one recollection
of an incident with his father, Brent said:

BRENT: He was always critical of me . . . Always! I felt worthless in his eyes and after a time I became convinced that I was worthless! I wanted to scream, "NO! I don't deserve this!" But I never did . . . And now . . . when Brandon screams at me I see my father! I hear my father! . . . It's like Brandon IS MY FATHER! And I feel the same rage toward him that I felt toward my father . . . and then I feel that this time it will be different! This time I will stop him from screaming at me . . . I'll stop him . . . no matter what it takes!

As Brent spoke, he became increasingly tearful, and Sue held his hand. At the end of the above sequence he burst into tears, and Sue moved close and hugged him as he cried in her arms. Over the next few sessions with Brent and Sue, Brent became able to allow himself to become vulnerable as he became aware of his loneliness and shame that came from years of his father's verbal and emotional treatment of him. He became aware of a new sense of shame over the way he treated his son. This shame was tempered by his hope that he could change his response to his son, repair their relationship, and discover himself and his son anew. This took a number of sessions and was not as easy as he had hoped. His son was slower to trust him and open up to him than he expected. He struggled not to get angry with his son for not forgiving him on Brent's time frame. With Sue and Alice serving as his attachment figures, Brent gradually came to accept his son's mistrust, to accept his son, and to win him over with patience, understanding, and empathy.

It is not safe for a child to explore themes in a session when there is a likelihood that her parents will react to her words and behaviors in a way that increases her underlying sense of shame or fear. For this reason, the DDP therapist delays joint sessions until first having confidence that the parents will be able to support the presence of safety for the child in the session (as discussed in detail in Chapter 4).

COREGULATION

It is common practice to encourage parents and teachers to stay calm when a child is angry. This recommendation is paired with the statement that if the adult also becomes angry, the child's anger will likely escalate. Which is true. However, there is a middle way that promotes better coregulation.

The emotion of anger (and all emotions for that matter) is expressed in the body, being evident in the person's facial expressions, voice tone and intensity, gestures, and posture. The bodily expression of an emotion is defined as the affect. Affect is not considered to be the emotion but rather is the sign that an emotion exists. For example, we are able to affectively match a child's expression of their emotion without experiencing the emotion myself. In doing so, we are often able to coregulate the child's emotion, much like the parent does with their infant. When the infant is agitated, the parent tends to increase the intensity and pitch of his vocalizations, while rocking the infant a little more quickly. The parent is matching the energy of the infant by being increasingly animated without being agitated.

EXAMPLE OF COREGULATION

JUDY [16-YEAR-OLD]: [Yells] You can't help me! You don't know anything about me!

ANNE [THERAPIST]: [Matching Judy's intensity] If I don't know you . . . of course I can't help you! Would you help me? Would you help me to get to know you a bit?

Anne might have responded instead with a quiet expression of empathy:

ANNE: It would be hard to talk with me if you thought that I don't know you.

This might well lead to the response:

JUDY: Dah! Isn't that what I said! You really are so lame!

If Judy responded to the therapist's expression of empathy in this way, there is a good chance that her response is related to the therapist not having matched Judy's affect. This mismatch of affective states often leads to the child experiencing the therapist as not really "getting it."

Matching the child's affective expression of an emotion helps the child to experience the therapist's empathy nonverbally. When parent's match their infant's affective expressions, they do so without words. And this often is central to the infant's remaining or becoming regulated. Such matching creates the synchrony that is often present in those lovely parent–infant interactions. The same synchrony enables the infant and parent to remain focused on the same activity or object together as they take turns in their serve and return cycles.

Matching affect is not only reserved for anger. The child who is expressing sadness is often soothed by the therapist's voice and slow, gentle movements. The child with symptoms consistent with ADHD often becomes more regulated and less agitated when the therapist is engaged with more animation and a quicker than usual rhythm.

Matching affective states often emerges naturally in good conversations between friends. When at the initial stages of the session you focus on matching the child's affective expressions of his emotions, you are creating a relational synchrony where a good conversation may emerge.

You may try to maintain a therapeutic atmosphere by relating in a fairly relaxed manner to set the other person at ease. This is often how you communicate empathy for the other's experience. But when the client's expressions show a much higher degree of intensity, from anger, agitation, confusion, or frustration, the client may feel unheard if you do not match their intensity. Or it may seem that you are "not real" because you are in the role of a therapist and not demonstrating a more natural response, like a friend might show.

It is important to remember that matching affect is the middle way. If you react emotionally to the child's emotions, then there is a risk of increasing dysregulation or control battles. There also is the risk that your emotional reactivity will undermine the child's confidence in you. The child may sense that you are not emotionally strong enough to remain centered when the child needs you to be. The key is to match the child's affective expression of their emotion, not match the emotion itself.

AFTER MATCHING, THEN LEAD TOWARD HIDDEN OR MORE VULNERABLE EMOTIONS

The emotion of anger is often a defensive emotion, hiding more vulnerable emotions underneath. For example, anger may cover over a child's sense of fear, shame, sadness, or loneliness. Anger protects the child from the vulnerability of the other emotions. With vulnerability, the child is showing a need to rely on you or his parent, and many children are not willing to rely on anyone. With anger, they do not need to rely on anyone. Anger gives a sense of strength and self-reliance, though this sense of strength may be fragile and is often maintained with rigid defensiveness.

If you are able to match the affective expression of the child's anger, a synchronized rhythm emerges that tends to have a momentum that maintains their interaction. At its best, the initiatives and responses of you and the child are seamless, and the momentum of the conversation causes it to continue.

Once this momentum is attained, with you and the child in a similar affective state, you are likely to be able to gradually lead the affective expressions to change to reflect the affective expressions of other emotions. Thus, you might first match the affective expression of the child's anger, then when you sense the developing synchrony and momentum, you gradually express the affective expressions of uncertainty and then disappointment and finally sadness that are likely present under the anger. Often the child is then aware of her own sadness as she remains synchronized in her expressions with the therapist.

This process is evident in the following example:

John, 12 years old, is one of Steve and Rachel's sons. He has a 14-year-old brother, Kenneth. John challenges his parent's rules routinely, often with angry outbursts, and then retreats to his room. John and his parents seldom engage in relaxing conversations. This is the fourth session with the family, the second with John and his parents together. The therapist, Nathan, had moved the focus of their conversation from John's camping trip with his friend Abe and Abe's parents to his return home and reluctance to tell his parents anything about the trip.

> **NATHAN:** You were just telling us about your two days with Abe at the State Park, John, and I'm wondering why you didn't tell your parents about these things when they asked you over the past few days.

JOHN: I was telling you, not them! And I didn't tell them before either because they're really not interested. They're just glad that I was gone so there weren't any problems at home. They don't like me around!

NATHAN: Oh, John! How hard that is if they don't seem to want you around!

JOHN: It's been that way for so long I don't even notice it anymore!

NATHAN: That long! So, this is not something new!

JOHN: As long as I can remember . . . from the first time they realized I wasn't as great as Kenneth! He's so wonderful and they figure that I'll never be as smart and friendly and "good" as he is! It sucks!

NATHAN: [All along matching the intense affect of John's anger] So it seems that he's the good one . . . and it seems that you're . . .

JOHN: Yeah, that's right, just say it! I'm the bad one! The one that never should have been born!

NATHAN: Never born!! Never born! Oh, John . . . John [gradually reducing intensity, longer pauses] . . . John . . . it seems to you that . . . that your parents see you . . . see you . . . as the bad one . . . and even that . . . [almost a whisper] they might not want you . . . not want you . . . to be their son.

JOHN: [As quiet as the therapist] They don't . . . [voice cracking] They don't.

NATHAN: [Still very gentle and slow] It seems . . . seems . . . like they don't want you . . . don't want you.

John is now crying, covering his face, and looking toward the window.

Nathan has a few tears. After a minute he tells John that unless he would rather Nathan not talk with his parents now about what he said, he would do so in order to hear what they have to say. John did not respond, and Nathan turned to Steve and Rachel and used John's words so that they heard again his experience. They responded with empathy and tears as well and expressed gratitude that John told them how things seemed to him even though it must have been very hard. They acknowledged their many conflicts, going back a number of months, and expressed a commitment to both reduce them and also find ways to communicate their love for him in spite of the disagreements. Nathan asked John if he wanted to answer them or if it would be ok for Nathan to answer them for him. John said Nathan could answer for him.

NATHAN: [Speaking for John] I want to believe you! I really do! But it's hard. I get into trouble all the time and Kenneth hardly ever does—and everyone likes him. I try . . . I really do . . . but it never seems like it's good enough. I worry that you're going to give up on me.

STEVE: I get why you'd think that we love Kenneth more than you . . . I really do . . . He always does seem to do what we want him to, and we don't argue much. And you, John . . . you're more like I was when I was your age . . . and I was convinced that my parents didn't want me either.

JOHN: You and gran and grandpa fought all the time?

STEVE: About as much as we do with you.

JOHN: What happened to make things better?

STEVE: I grew up, they grew up. Grandpa realized that I was like him when he was my age.

JOHN: Really? [surprised and a bit amused]

STEVE: Yeah, weird, huh?

JOHN: [Smiles] So does this mean that . . . you're ready to grow up more?

STEVE: [Smiles] It does, and I am.

This session was a turning point in the therapy. They managed to take a step toward repair of their relationship, which seemed to give them confidence that they could handle conflicts better in the future. And they did . . . sometimes, with increasing frequency over the next six months, at which point they took a break from therapy.

As the momentum of the therapeutic conversation unfolds, the child will often follow the therapist into a more vulnerable emotional state if the therapist has first matched the affective expressions of the child's defenses against vulnerability and then nonverbally leads him into the underlying emotions by affectively giving expression to those emotions.

REGULATION FIRST

Just as is the case in human development, safety needs to be present in therapy before exploration can proceed. Attachment theory and research demonstrate that the young child's first priority is to feel safe. With safety, the child begins to trust that his parents will be there for him when he needs them to be. After that, the child is safe to explore. You, as the therapist, need to be aware of this sequence as well. Is the child feeling safe enough that he is now able to explore a difficult challenge in his life?

The factor to consider is whether or not the child demonstrates sufficient emotional regulation to engage in exploration.

The first signs of emotional distress and possible dysregulation that you need to be aware of are, of course, nonverbal. She begins to fidget, her voice becomes a bit agitated, her face becomes tense. Then she might change the topic or use words to indicate that she is becoming bored or annoyed talking about the theme. You need to be sensitive and responsive to those signs rather than continuing with the discussion as if the child had not shown any distress. Ignoring signs of emotional distress is likely to make the child feel trapped in the conversation, intensify her efforts to stop it, and avoid entering into such conversations in the future.

It would be better for you to engage in the call and response cycle. Using this technique, you would modify the exploration in response to the child's signs that the exploration is stressful. That does not mean that you would immediately stop exploring that theme and change the topic. Trying to avoid eliciting any signs of distress is likely reduce the likelihood that therapy will address and integrate stressful themes. Rather you might:

1. Pause and reflect a bit on the conversation to that point:
    "So, it seems like you were a bit surprised when your mom seemed to change her mind. You didn't know what was going on."
2. Reduce the emotional intensity of the conversation. With less energy in your voice, the child's emotional experience might become less intense and easier to regulate. Focus on being reflective, not evoking affect.
3. Lead the conversation to focus more on gathering facts and less on how the child experienced what happened.
    "Before you came home and saw your mom, what

were you doing at your friend's house? Do you do that a lot? Do you both enjoy that a lot?"

4. Lead the conversation toward other related events or relationships, looking for similarities and differences. This will help the child to step back from that immediate event and take a view that involves more context.

5. Quietly summarize the conversation you are having with the child to the parent. This will give the child a break from the conversation while also moving it into a more reflective—and less affective—experience.

All of these interventions may reduce the emotional experience of the conversation. Your focus now is on wondering about, not reexperiencing, the events that are being explored. Experiencing less emotion, the child might be ready and able to continue to explore the event.

During the course of this therapeutic conversation, you are always monitoring the need to coregulate the child's emotional experience to maintain the child's safety so that she is able to engage in the cocreation of a more healing and integrative story. Coregulation must precede, and proceed along with, cocreation!

ACCEPTANCE OF ALL EMOTIONS

Our emotions are an aspect of our sense of self, and, like all aspects of self, when we are able to accept their presence, we are more able to integrate them into the other core aspects of ourselves. When we evaluate our emotions, believing them to be right or wrong, we tend to risk losing our ability to regulate them. When our anger is experienced as being wrong, its presence and expression may activate the following reactions:

1. We become defensive about being angry and tend to stub-

bornly insist that we have a "right" to be angry, justifying it over other possible responses we might have to the situation.

2. We rigidly protect our angry stance, being ready to become aggressive toward those who try to control it.

3. In justifying our anger, we do not consider why we became angry and we are not able to explore the situation openly or in a way that might invalidate our angry interpretation.

4. If we are angry in spite of the fact that we believe that anger is wrong, our anger might trigger shame about our reaction, and the shame may activate further anger.

5. After our angry outburst, our defensive or shame-based experience of it often persists, making it very difficult to explore it safely for ways to manage it more effectively.

6. If our anger is "bad," we are more likely to experience it as something separate from us, something that opposes us, and something that we are unable to control.

7. We lose the meaning of our anger, so we are not able to learn from it and explore other, more adaptive responses to the event that evoked it.

By accepting our emotions as neither right nor wrong, we are more able to use them to discover our wishes, our priorities, our values, and our conflicts. While the behavior that is associated with anger might be inappropriate, or "wrong," the emotion itself is not. The emotion provides us with an alert for how we might want to address challenging situations and increase our opportunities for desirable ones. By accepting our emotions, we are more able to notice how intense they are and thus have a better sense of how important something is to us. Mindfulness, as described in Chapter 8, may be useful for both clients and therapists to practice to assist with this process.

It is crucial that therapists adopt the stance that emotions convey meanings and that they serve as a guide for assisting an individual in making sense of his challenging behaviors so he can be in a better position to develop a coherent story that will guide future patterns of behavior. Instead of focusing on "managing" or extinguishing the emotion, it may well serve the child better if he can understand its meaning and its implications for other aspects of his life.

What might his anger, fear, sadness, shame mean?

1. He has had difficult experiences in the past that he has not come to understand and resolve. He may have avoided thinking about them and is now repeating—again and again—behaviors secondary to those unresolved events.

2. His emotional reaction to a current event or person may directly relate to its association with a similar event or person in his past that he has not managed to understand and resolve.

3. His emotion may relate to being ambivalent about a person or event. He is not able to explore the fact that what he thinks he "should" think and feel is different from what he actually thinks and feels.

4. A particular emotion may not be welcome in the child's sense of self. For example, if the child thinks being sad means he is a "baby," then situations that might naturally evoke a sense of sadness are likely to be avoided or to increase the risk of dysregulation. If he cannot avoid a sad experience, he might react to it with a rigid alternative emotion—anger—or be overwhelmed by it and move into a sense of despair.

While sometimes your curious and accepting attitude toward the child's emotion enables the child to accept it as well and openly explore it, at other times this is not sufficient. The child rejects you, resists any exploration, and withdraws from you. At the first sign that the emotional state is not being accepted, you need to accept this and explore that rather than the original emotion.

LAUGHTER AND JOY

Within safe relationships, there is great opportunity for the joint experience of laughter and joy. When children have had difficulties regulating their negative emotions of anger, sadness, or fear, they most often also have difficulty regulating their positive emotions, such as joy, excitement, love, and happiness. Those emotions often create anxiety—the child does not trust that they will last. Often, too, they do not see anything in their lives worth laughing about. In these situations, when the child has had success regulating her negative emotions, she still may need assistance in both feeling safe enough to not inhibit the experiences of laughter and joy and also help regulating positive feelings as they emerge.

Laughter is a spontaneous expression that may make a person feel exposed and open to ridicule. Individuals who have not felt safe with others may have inhibited such spontaneous expressions of humor and delight for fear of a negative evaluation. They may have developed a habit of inhibiting any acts of self-expression that would attract attention.

Your efforts to help children and their parents to move into more positive emotional states begins with your confidence that they have reasons—no matter how few—to laugh and trust emerging experiences of happiness.

Valuing all aspects of your client's experiences, not just the challenges he has, will leave time and space in your reciprocal conversations with them for positive experiences to emerge. Your joining them—intersubjectively— in their positive experiences will make those experiences deeper and more lasting.

Being open to the silver lining in difficult experiences may help the child to remain open to other positive experiences. Modeling and supporting a sense of humor in spite of difficulties is likely to be helpful. That does not mean minimizing negative experiences or trying to talk someone out of their discouragement. Rather it means leaving room to see the edges of these experiences when the child is ready to do so.

If you practice attachment-focus therapy, you convey a strong and clear acceptance of the child's experiences. Your persistent acceptance of his emotional life will likely facilitate his acceptance of himself. He will likely become able to face his "problems" and "mistakes" without going into shame about himself. With such self-acceptance the child will likely become more open to joyful experiences. He will likely become grateful for positive opportunities and events that he is now able to experience more fully. He will likely come to cherish positive experiences within the family, feeling confident that if conflicts arise, the family will have the ability to repair their relationships. Again, because of the value of your intersubjective presence, when you are able to experience joy over developmental changes in the functioning of the child and family, they are also likely to experience joy in how far they have come and what they have experienced their family as being able to be.

EMOTIONAL CONVERSATIONS

Emotions are embedded in good conversations. There may be laughter and silliness, wondering and exploring, tales of enchantment and sorrow, as well as light meandering from one surprising, routine, unusual, and/or puzzling event to the next. Sometimes the conversation is just about sharing whatever enters the minds of all who are engaged. Because you are interested in the minds of each other, anything and everything becomes interesting.

Often in attachment-based family sessions, the initial goal is simply to have this sort of emotional conversation about whatever will create an open, engaged, relaxed, and connected attitude, building safety and an experience of sharing. Many families have forgotten about this type of experience because they have become lost in differences, conflicts, anger, and isolation. Coming back to having conversations with one another, they are more likely to find that their relationships—family—is stronger than whatever conflicts emerge.

Anything and everything needs to be safe to share and explore within these conversations. Some families are not so sure about this and may say some of the following things:

FAMILY MEMBER: *We don't talk about that.*

THERAPIST: Sometimes that happens in a family—certain things are "off limits." And then they're not addressed, and they just get bigger and stop you from getting it right and keep you from being close! I can show you how to talk about that in a way that really helps you all.

FAMILY MEMBER: *He needs to stop doing that and do what is right.*

THERAPIST: We can figure out how to sort out differences without one being right and the other being wrong. My job is to help families find how what is best for one can also be best for all. Sometimes that's hard!

FAMILY MEMBER: *Why won't she just do what we say?*

THERAPIST: Great question! We can figure that out! And we need to begin by understanding so many things about what each of you thinks, feels, hopes, and dreams. We don't solve the puzzle by studying one piece! We get to know all the pieces and then the place for each piece will be much easier to see!

FAMILY MEMBER: *Talk, talk, talk! We need to see some change! Talking about it doesn't help anything!*

THERAPIST: Seems like you're worried that he doesn't really mean what he says. You're not so sure that you can trust him that he really wants to work on this. If that's your worry, thanks for letting us know! That's where we have to begin! What would it mean if he does not want to work on this? Would it mean that you that your relationship is not that important to him? If that's so, what is that like for you? I'd guess it would be very hard if you're not important to your son.

FAMILY MEMBER: *Why bother? What I think is really not important to her.*

THERAPIST: If that's so, it would be hard to talk about this stuff! It would be hard to be together, to feel like a family. And we have to make sense of that—why would your thoughts not be important to your daughter/mom? And if it's not so . . . if what you think *is* important to her but something else is getting in the way . . . it would be horrible to give up on each other because we missed what the issue really was! That's why I push so hard for us to figure out what's going on! So we get it right! And then maybe we can figure out what to do that is best for each of you and all of you.

FAMILY MEMBER: *That's it! I'm done.*

THERAPIST: Oh my! How painful that must be to want to give up on your relationship with your son/dad. I know that over the years you were close [or you wanted so much to figure out a way to be closer]! And now to feel that there is no hope . . . how painful that must be . . . I have to find a way . . . to help you all to get that hope back! I have to find a way to help you to see that there is still reason to have hope! We just have to find what it is! And that's what I have to do . . . find a reason for hope . . . a reason we can trust! A reason for trying again to make the family work!

To have conversations that "work" to build safety, connections, and joint discoveries within the family, the family needs to be able to understand and accept the emotions that emerge as the family members begin to speak openly with each other. This will be a rocky ride. You need to take the lead in learning the best path to take for each particular family and this particular moment in their history. The emotions that emerge along this journey are our guides as to how to navigate, when to pause and address the obstacles before going forward, when to check the gas and oil, and when to reflect on whether the emerging destination is where we all want to go. And you need to take the lead in ensuring that the emotions are seen, accepted, and regulated. Then all family members will be safe and engaged in discovering the best path to take for them all.

ATTACHMENT-BASED RECOMMENDATIONS TO GIVE TO PARENTS REGARDING FACILITATING EMOTIONAL REGULATION

1. Your child's emotions do not become regulated alone. His emotions tend to become synchronized with your emotions. When your emotions are regulated, your infant's emotions naturally synchronize with them and are regulated as well. This is the most important skill for you to have if you wish to help your child to become emotionally regulated. Your child will not become regulated emotionally if you are habitually frightened, angry, agitated, or in despair when you are with her. The infants with the most significant attachment difficulties are those whose parents express anger or fear in response to their infant's rage or terror.

2. It is easy to see why your dysregulated emotional states will make it difficult for your child to develop emotional regulation. It is less obvious that when you remain calm and detached when your child expresses intense emotions, your child is also at risk of becoming dysregulated. Your child needs the affective expressions of her emotional states to be coregulated with your regulated affective states. When you are expressing little or no affect, your child experiences her emotions alone, and when they become intense, they may lead to dysregulation.

3. Coregulating your child's anger does not mean that you need to match his anger, which could lead to escalation of anger for both of you. Coregulation of your child's anger means that you match the nonverbal—affective—expression of his anger. Your child's anger is evident in the intensity and pitch of his voice and the stern expression of his face. When you match this intensity—without becoming angry yourself—your child often experiences your response as signifying "I get it! I know how angry you are!" Knowing that you "get it" while still accepting your child often calms your child and helps him to stay regulated.

4. Anger, fear, sadness, jealousy, excitement, joy, and shame are emotions. They are neither good nor bad, they just are. Emotions signal the meaning of an event to us. Does it make us feel safe or is it a threat to our safety? Is it enjoyable or not, desirable or not? Emotions are a reflection of your child's inner life, and it is good for you and your child to know what they are! You might put restrictions on certain behaviors that express an emotion, but it is wise not to evaluate the emotion itself.

For example, if you say that it is ok for your child to be angry at you and then turn around and call his anger "disrespectful" that may send the message that it really isn't ok for her to be angry at you. Instead, you might want to say that her anger is ok but her behavior is disrespectful. What behavior will you say is disrespectful? Raising his voice? Speaking with some intensity in his voice and having a stern facial expression? Yet these are our body's natural ways to express anger. To smile and quietly say that you are angry is fake, and then your child might be in trouble for being fake. While certain words (swearing, name calling, threats) might be behaviors that are inappropriate for expressing anger, nonverbal expressions are a natural part of a healthy expression of anger.

5. Reason is probably not of much value when responding to your child's emotional expressions. If she expresses sadness or fear and you try to reassure her or provide her with information to make the emotion go away, you are likely to make the emotion stronger. If the emotion is a signal of how your child is experiencing a situation, it is better to explore the situation as to its meaning rather than to try to turn off the signal. Responding to the emotional expression with PACE is more likely to help you and your child understand the situation. Responding to your child's emotion with empathy is likely to reduce the intensity of the emotion more than any reassurance or argument will. Empathy indicates that the emotional signal was understood and now there is less need for it. The distress was shared and is now easier to handle.

6. As is the case for most situations in which you want to have an influence on your child, your own ways of understanding and expressing your emotions and then integrating them into your decisions and behavior will influence how well your child is able to do the same with his emotions. If you pretend that you are not sad or worried when you are, you are modeling this as a way for your child to deal with his emotions. This is not to say that you rely on your child for support, but rather that you acknowledge that you are sad or worried and then you act in ways that are the best ways for you to deal with the situation that is associated with those emotions.

DISCIPLINE

Situations in which you need to discipline your child to help him develop his socialization skills are likely to be some of the more challenging situations for emotional regulation. The following principles are likely to make discipline more effective:

1. Setting limits on your child's behavior or expecting behaviors from your child that he does not want to do are likely to place stress on the relationship. Having a strong relationship (connection) will help your child to trust your motives for having the expectation (correction). If most of your interactions with your child involve mutual enjoyment or support, the few interactions involving discipline will be experienced within the bigger context. If conflicts over discipline are becoming repetitive, this may reflect the need to attend to your relationship (nurture connection). Correction is more effective when it occurs within the context of a strong connection.

2. The most effective discipline involves two hands. The first hand of discipline refers to the behavioral expecation. It is best that your expectation be clear and that you follow through to ensure that your expectation is met. Sometimes your child will not comply, and the consequence that follows is not effective or evokes a strong reaction from your child. In this circumstance, it is important to have the second hand of discipline available. This hand focuses on making sense of your child's opposition—why is he so opposed to meeting your expectation? This hand is greatly aided by holding an attitude of PACE while you try to make sense of what is motivating your child at that moment. Enforcing an expectation with empathy tends to be more effective than enforcing one with anger. Empathy makes your motives clear—the conflict you are having has to do with his behavior. Anger makes your motives confusing—might the conflict involve your relationship with your child or something negative about him?

3. At times repetitive discipline "problems" reflect that your child might have too much "freedom" or unstructured, unsupervised time to do what he wants. In this case, rather than providing a specific consequence for a specific behavior, it might be of greater value to provide one general consequence, namely, increased structure and supervision in his life. This needs to be given as a "gift" that will enable him to have greater success, not as a "punishment." Your attitude will often be crucial if your child is to accept the tighter daily rules.

4. You might consider how important it is to you that your child accepts the behavioral expectation that you have of her. If you are comfortable with her continuing to do what you wish she would not do, and she accepts the natural consequence for what she is doing, then this might be the easiest way for her to learn to make a different choice. If you think the behavior is too serious and needs to stop now, then it might be wise to increase the structure and supervision to make it much harder for her to engage in that behavior. Simply increasing the severity of the consequences for the behavior is often ineffective and also damages the trust that you want her to have in your motives and the relationship.

5. Using relationship withdrawal as a means of discipline (isolation or giving him the cold shoulder) is not likely to be effective and may undermine your child's faith that the relationship is important to you. He needs to trust completely that the relationship is more important than the conflict. Isolation makes it impossible for him to rely on you to coregulate his distress over the limitation or expectation. When there is a conflict, there needs to be relationship repair, rather than distance and pretending nothing happened, as soon as you are both ready to engage in the process.

6. You are limiting your child's behavior, not trying to invalidate her experience! You get it—he really does not like spending Saturday afternoon at grandmother's house with you. He gets it—it is important to you that he go with you to grandmother's house. As long as you "get it," he's more likely to accept your directive, having some confidence that what he wants is important to you and is likely to influence your future decisions about how he might spend some of his Saturday afternoons. In this instance, your decision is based on your value about family responsibility, not on your desire to make him unhappy nor your insistence that he agree with your value.

In the next chapter, we will explore our final developmental area—reflective functioning—which is facilitated by a secure attachment and is very important to mental well-being.

chapter seven

Developing Reflective Functioning

At times, therapists take reflective functioning for granted, and we only notice when it is absent. Here is one example:

Todd was a 28-year-old man who sought treatment because he had difficulty knowing what he wanted in his life. After obtaining his college degree, he couldn't decide what sort of career he would pursue. Also, while he said that he liked a number of the women he was dating, he had no idea if and why he might choose to commit to a long-term relationship with any of them. He said that he was not satisfied with his life, but he did not know how he might change it so that he would be more satisfied. Todd's therapist asked him to write a brief biography of his life. He was told to relate whatever experiences that he saw as having been important to him for whatever reason, such as they were interesting, difficult, an adventure, a loss, exciting, or painful. Two weeks later, Todd returned with this biography and indicated that the therapist could read the six pages then if he wanted. After reading through it once, the therapist

was confused and asked if he could read it a second time. Todd
had described many events that had occurred, primarily in his
adolescent and young adult years. But he did not describe his
experience of any of those events. His parents had divorced, a
college friend had died, he rode his motorcycle across the country
with another friend, he had traveled to Italy, he had bought an
old house and fixed it up over a two-year period of time. Never
once did Todd mention that he had been excited, worried, sad,
proud, confused, angry, happy, or regretful. It was as if he was
an objective reporter who regarded his life but did not live it.

The difficulties that Todd had in describing his experiences
in his biography were repeated many times in therapy. Todd
did not show many reflective functioning skills. It was hard
for him to describe, or possibly even be aware of, his wishes,
thoughts, feelings, and intentions about the many events that
had occurred over the course of his life. When his therapist
asked him detailed questions about specific events, Todd was
excellent at providing whatever details were requested—about
the facts, about what was external to him. He paused and
seemed confused when asked how something affected him, how
he made sense of things, how things might have impacted him.
He was aware of his exterior life, but not his inner life.

One reason for Todd's lack of any description of his experience
may have been that his parents did not reflect about the meanings of his actions when they interacted with him. They may have
failed to sufficiently and accurately make sense of his behaviors
during their interactions or the events of his infancy. They may
have failed to show sufficient interest in what his behavior repre-
sented with regard to his wishes, desires, and intentions.

We emphasized in both Chapter 2 and Chapter 6 how central attachment is for the development of the infant's emotional

regulation skills. And rightfully so! In secure relationships, the parent frequently coregulates the infant's intense emotional experience, and gradually the toddler has the capacity to self-regulate her emotions. At the same time, the sensitive parent is making sense of the events—internal or external—that elicited the infant's intense emotion. As the parent makes sense of the infant's emotions, she is communicating: "No worries," "That was a loud noise wasn't it? It was scary," and "You so wanted to play with the cat now, and the cat doesn't want to play with you! You really seem sad now." As the parent engages again and again in making sense of the infant's nonverbal expressions through associating them with events in the child's life, the infant comes more and more to anticipate that the parent will help him to make sense of what is happening. Over time, the infant and toddler begin to actively participate in this sense-making activity. The parent is engaged in the process of making meaning of the events and expressions of the child's life. In fundamental ways, the parent is constructing—or even creating—the meaning of what is happening. With time the infant is coconstructing—or cocreating—these meanings with the parents.

When we are able to try to understand the meanings of our own behavior and the behaviors of others and make sense of these behaviors, we are engaged in reflective functioning. We then may think and say with confidence that we did something because we were sad or angry, because we were hoping to accomplish something, or because we were distracted. We might also infer why our friend, parent, or partner did something, having a hunch about what they were thinking, feeling, or intending. Some conflicts occur because we are convinced that our reflective functioning was accurate even when the other person explains that it was not. This process occurs again and again within our minds and the minds of others, focusing on ourselves and others.

While Todd's therapist may believe Todd when he says that he does not know what he thinks or feels or wants, most often others do not. When he fails to give a "satisfactory" answer to a question about his thoughts, feelings, and intentions, his colleague or friend may challenge him for not being honest, for making an excuse, and, if he is telling the truth, for not thinking seriously enough about the consequences of his behavior.

Too often, parents, teachers, or therapists ask a child, "Why did you do that?" the child replies "I don't know!" and this is followed by "Of course you know! That's an excuse. You're going to sit there until you tell me." What if he does not know? Given what we know about the impact of insecure relationships, he may not have the developmental capacity to reflect on his behaviors and motivations. There is a good chance that a child who has experienced chronic stress in his life truly does not have the answer. If his parents were facing many stresses during his early years and thus did not express interest in his emotional life very often, he may not know much about his emotions. There is also a good chance that a child who has experienced an acutely stressful event does not know what he feels, thinks, or wants, nor what led him to engage in a questionable behavior. Our reflective functioning may be slow to develop when under chronic stress and may not be engaged at all when under acute stress.

We therapists might do well to consider the possibility that just as children may need our help to coregulate their emotional states, they may also need our help to cocreate the meaning of their behaviors and the behaviors of others. Just as problems may be much easier to address when the child's regulation skills improve, so too are they easier to address when the child's reflective functioning improves. Given this, we might think about which of the following sequences is likely to be the most therapeutic:

1. **THERAPIST:** What's that about?

    CHILD: I don't know.

    THERAPIST: I think you do know. Take your time and tell me.

2. **THERAPIST:** What's that about?

    CHILD: I don't know.

    THERAPIST: That must be hard, not knowing why that happened . . . what you were thinking . . . what she was thinking. Makes it hard not knowing what to do if that happens again. How about we try to figure it out—you're clever, I'm clever. What might it be?

The first sequence suggests that the child is holding back from you something that he knows. It places pressure on the child to say what he must be thinking, even if the pressure is lessened by "take your time." This is often experienced as being intrusive, placing yourself into his private, inner world without being invited.

The second sequence involves no judgment about the child's statement that he does not know (acceptance). It then involves the process of wondering about the event/behaviors (curiosity). Throughout, the therapist is sensitive to the child's emerging experience of a stressful event (empathy).

REGULATION PRECEDES REFLECTIVE FUNCTIONING

Therapeutic conversations are about our experiences of the events of our lives. These conversations hopefully lead us toward understanding our experiences more fully and/or changing our experiences. These experiences have an affective and a reflective component to them. The affective involves how our emotions are associated with the events, while the reflective involves how we make sense of the events. If our memory of an event evokes emotions that lead to dysregulation, we are likely to avoid those memories, or if we do try to recall the events, we tend to have difficulty making sense of them in a flexible or more integrative manner.

When attempting to enhance a child's reflective functioning, the first priority is to ensure his emotional regulation while exploring the events. If fear or shame is associated with the events, he may become dysregulated, dissociated, angry, or avoidant in response to efforts to explore the events. Issues of emotional dysregulation and how to address them (explored in Chapter 6) will need to be considered before making any efforts to cocreate new meanings of the events. PACE is often helpful in reducing the fear or shame of the experience so that the conversation can proceed in a reflective manner. At the first sign that emotions associated with an event are being activated, the therapist attends to and coregulates those emotions. For example:

Jane was a 10-year-old girl who was described as being irritable and oppositional with her parents over the past few months. When her parents asked her about what was happening, she would become angry and then run to her room, often in tears. Her parents said that this was "out of character" for Jane, and they had no idea as to what might be going on for her. The following sequence occurred when the therapist gently led the conversation to a recent event when Jane had told her parents that she was tired of them telling her what to do and that she could decide things by herself:

> **THERAPIST:** And I heard that Sunday was a lot harder than Saturday for you! I think that your parents said that it might

be time to get your homework done and that you got kind of upset about that!

JANE: I know that I have homework, and I don't need to be reminded! I should be able to do it when I feel like it!

THERAPIST: Ah! So, it seems to you that you're old enough to handle your homework on your own.

JANE: I am, but they think I'm a baby! I don't want to talk about this!

THERAPIST: Ah! It seems to you like . . .

JANE: I said don't want to talk about this!

THERAPIST: [turning to Jane's parents, speaking with a slow, quiet, and soothing voice] I am glad that Jane told us that she would rather not talk about this now. This is a very hard thing to talk about—having conflicts or disagreements in the family. And she does not know me . . . she might even think that I'll be on your side and say that she shouldn't have said that to you. Do you understand, and are you ok with that?

MOM: Yes, of course. I know that this is hard to talk about.

THERAPIST: Probably for you too! When a kid and her parents have been close over the years and then they start having some disagreements, it is hard for everyone. How do we stay close when we disagree?

DAD: That's why we're seeing you, so you can help us to figure that out.

THERAPIST: I'm glad that you both understand. You're asking a lot of your daughter to come here and talk about your family struggles with me.

JANE: It's your fault! You made me mad!

THERAPIST: Ah, Jane, your saying that it seems to you that your parents caused this struggle! If they hadn't told you to remember your homework none of this would have happened.

JANE: Yeah, why do they treat me like a baby?

Jane then became engaged in the conversation about the conflict they had. Her probable shame about her outburst was met with understanding and acceptance, normalizing how hard these conflicts can be for everyone in the family. With the shame being coregulated, she was able to start making sense of what happened. Jane's inference about her parent's motives, that they saw her as immature, could then be explored with the understanding that of course she would be upset if her parents viewed her "like a baby."

Shame certainly interferes with the development of our reflective functioning. We are not likely to wonder, "Why did I do that?" or "Why did my dad do that?" if we believe that the most likely reason for the event is that we are bad, lazy, selfish, or unlovable. Shame carries the assumption that we are worthless and that any problem, conflict, disappointment, or mistake involves a core deficiency in our self. Shame is not about our behavior, it is about our self. We might be able to change our behavior and hence repair a relationship. We are not likely to be able to repair the relationship if the problem relates to our core self.

Most of us experience a sense of shame periodically when something goes wrong. Most often we are able to explore the origins of the shame, identify a behavior or circumstance, understand it as being a mistake that can be fixed or a behavior that can be changed. We are able to think it through with a bit of self-compassion and acceptance and realize that we are not perfect. We are able to accept what happened, learn from it, and get it right the next time.

PERVASIVE SHAME

But when our shame is pervasive, this process is much more difficult. We lack confidence that it is only a mistake, which we can learn from. We see the event or our behavior as representing a flaw in ourself. When this is the case, we do not want to think about it. We tend to shield ourselves from the experience of shame through denial, excuses, blaming someone else, minimizing, or rage at the person who is addressing what we have done. We don't learn from the mistake because we don't acknowledge that we made a mistake. We don't think about it, we don't reflect! We avoid using (and developing) our reflective functioning, which involves exploring what we or others think, want, and intend to do.

We all experience shame at times, but what makes it so pervasive that we stop wondering about our inner life? There may be a variety of factors:

1. Abuse or neglect. Experiencing abuse or neglect may result in a sense that we deserved such treatment—the only way to make sense of it is that we are bad or unlovable.

2. Chronic conflicts and criticisms. If the majority of the interactions with our parents are negative, we may come to believe that it must be our fault.

3. Conflict without relationship repair. If after a child's misbehavior, the parents employ relationship withdrawal as a disciplinary technique and do not talk with the child or show signs of enjoyment of him for a period of time, the message they send is that if the child wants a relationship

with a parent, the child needs to be "good." The relationship is conditional.

4. Loss of an important attachment relationship. When a parent abandons a child, or in some cases when a parent dies, the child may be convinced that it was their fault.

5. Parents react to their child's misbehavior with intense verbal criticism or emotional outbursts that verge on being dysregulated. If the parent is THAT angry, the child must really be bad.

6. Criticisms of the child are directed at his self, not his behavior. These messages include: you're bad; you never do anything right; you are so selfish; you just don't care; it always has to be your way; why are you so lazy? I have to love you but I don't have to like you.

Addressing the child's shame in therapy is a delicate process, since shame tends to activate social withdrawal or anger. Trying to talk a child out of his shame is likely to fail. He most likely will assume that you either do not know him well enough or you don't mean what you say or that it is your job to say that. The best responses to expressions of shame are likely to involve PACE. First, you might accept the experience, with empathy:

That must be so hard, if you think that you're just a bad kid! No wonder it's hard for you to think about this! It seems to you that it's always your fault and that you'll never get it right!

When you have a sense that the child trusts that you understand his experience of shame, you might follow with curiosity:

How long has it seemed like that to you, that you'll never change?

Are there times when you don't think that you're just no good?

Do you think that you might have started to feel this way about yourself after your dad left home and just seemed to disappear from your life?

With your acceptance, empathy, and curiosity—but without challenging his experience of himself, the child is likely to begin to question his experience. At some point he may ask if you experience him that way. Then, or if you sense that he is open to your experience, you might say:

I don't think that you're a bad kid. Though I know you think and feel that. I think that you get down on yourself a lot, find your anger getting big and aren't sure what to do about it, and often really feel alone. But I don't see you the way you see yourself. How you see yourself is more important than how I see you. I hope someday you see the things about you that I see.

FEAR

Another emotion that tends to compromise the development and use of reflective functioning is fear. If a memory of an event activates fear, we are not likely to think about it. If the event was traumatic, the memory of the event might be experienced as almost as terrifying as the event itself. Making sense of an event, or our own behavior, is likely to be avoided if it only frightens us again. In those circumstances, many children, and some adults, will refuse to talk about it.

Aversion to talking about a frightening incident from our

past is likely to be greater if we experienced the incident alone. If we were comforted and made safe at the time of the frightening incident or immediately afterwards, we will be much more open to exploring its meaning at a later date. If we try to face these terrors alone, we might become more intense and dysregulated; whereas if we face them with someone who keeps us safe, we are more likely to become calmer and more relaxed.

In therapy, when you believe that the child is having trouble engaging in reflective functioning because of fear of remembering and thinking about an event, you might acknowledge your experience of the child's fear, normalize it, and recognize her hesitancy to talk about something that was very upsetting and scary. This might be followed by suggesting that you only talk about part of it now and that she tell you when she has had enough. You might suggest that you summarize what you believe happened and that she let you know if what you say is correct or not. She might also want to write it down, draw a picture, or whisper to her parent what she thinks, and her parent will speak for her. You might also suggest that her original experience of fear might have really seemed hard because she was all alone with the feeling. If she shares it with someone who understands and comforts her, she might find that the fear is not so big and that it also gets smaller faster after talking about it.

Sometimes the child seems afraid over what she anticipates her parent thinks and feels about the incident. You might acknowledge this concern and express your belief that it would be good to know for sure what her parent might say. If the child still hesitates, you might suggest that you will ask the parent about the event because it is important for you to know and that the child can wait outside if she does not want to listen. Most children agree and stay. Those who leave tend to find a way to ask what the parent said when they were out of the room.

EXPERIENCES AND FACTS

As your clients become less and less defensive throughout their daily interactions with others, they increasingly discover that their relationships are able to thrive even when they include various differences. The key is that they are able to live a life where they routinely differentiate experiences from facts. When their partner or child expresses an experience different from their own, they often are able to respond with interest and curiosity rather than seeing it as a threat to their relationship. Defensiveness often results from our experiencing the other's expression of their inner life as their stating a fact. For example (John and Sue are partners):

> **SUE:** It seems to me that you don't enjoy spending time with me much anymore. When I suggest that we do something, you often have a reason not to and if you agree, it seems to be out of obligation.

> **JOHN:** How can you say that! Just last week we went out to eat twice. And you were worrying about your mother and I listened to you! I was planning to watch a movie on TV but I didn't even turn it on—I paid attention to everything you said.

> **SUE:** But I'm the one who usually has to initiate whatever we're doing.

> **JOHN:** You just beat me to it most of the time. And you tend to have specific things that you really want to do, and you bring them up, whereas I'm fine doing just about anything. I think you're reading too much into this, Sue.

In this example, Sue was describing her experience of her relationship with John, not facts. John replied with facts to prove that her experience was wrong. He chose to remind her of the things that they had done together, to see that the facts were on his side. He also had an explanation for why she initiated most of their times together—a matter of temperament—that has nothing to do with their relationship. Sue's experience wasn't validated. According to John, her experience was wrong! His explanations were not likely to change her experience of him not enjoying spending time with her.

If John had been able to understand that Sue was expressing her experience of him seeming to not enjoy spending as much time with her as he used to, his reply would have been something like:

> *Oh, Sue, I feel badly that I've given you that impression. If you feel that I don't enjoy being with you so much, I'd imagine that you might think that you're not that important to me. I am so sorry. I do enjoy being with you—a lot—and somehow I guess I've just not shown it as much as I've done in the past. Thanks a lot for letting me know! You are so special to me and I want you to know that! I hope that you believe me.*

In essence, John is saying that his feelings about Sue are different than her experience of what his feelings are. He feels sad that she experiences him as not enjoying being with her, and he wants to find ways to make his feelings about their relationship clearer.

The same applies to the parent–child relationship when the securely attached child is experiencing a stress in his confidence about what his mom feels about him.

JAKE [AGE 11]: Mom, I think that you're more proud of Matt [his 9-year-old brother] than you are of me! You get so excited when he does something well at school, you tell everyone about it! But when I do something well, it's like, "Ho, hum, no big deal anyway." Sometimes it even seems that you're disappointed in me.

MOM: Oh, Jake, I did not know that you felt that way! That would be so hard for you if you thought I was more proud of Matt than of you. And that I might even be disappointed in you! Thanks, so much for letting me know how you feel!

JAKE: Why do you get more excited about Matt than you do about me.

MOM: If I express my pride in him more than I do in you, maybe it's because he's had troubles with some of his courses lately and it seems to come easier for you. Or maybe because he's younger, and I sometimes forget that older kids want to feel valued just like younger kids do. If I haven't been as excited about you, I am sorry, Jake. I really am. I'm going to make it clear how proud I am of you, in all ways! And I'm not disappointed in you! I'm so glad you told me. I don't want you to ever doubt how proud and happy I am that you are my son!

If, however, she had experienced Jake's expressions as being statements of facts, she most likely would have attempted to protect herself and replied defensively:

MOM: Oh, Jake, that's not true! Of course I'm as proud of you as I am of Matt. You're just not around every time I brag about you. Or you might forget! Even if I do sing Matt's praises more than I speak about yours, you know that he has struggled more than you with his courses, and he needs it more—to keep him motivated. You don't need it so much, but it certainly does not mean that I'm disappointed in you.

Being able to separate a child's experiences from facts is a frequent result of developing the habit of seeing her inner life as being separate from her behavior, of reflecting on the child's thoughts, feelings, and wishes that might lead to her behaviors. When you always accept the inner life of the other—child or adult—you are more able to be curious about it without judgement and to understand it better, which enables you to understand their experience and use that understanding as a guide for your relationship. The child needs you to use your reflective functioning as much as they need to use their own.

When a person shares his experience about a problem or strain in your relationship with him, it is a gift—an opportunity to get busy repairing the relationship. There is no need for defensiveness when you are confident that the other is not stating a fact about you, but rather is sharing an experience about you or their relationship with you. There is no need for defensiveness when you trust that the other's motives involve a desire to strengthen the relationship, not end it.

Just as you benefit by not taking the other's expression of an experience as being an expression of fact, the same applies to your own experiences. When you experience your child's behavior, you may often assume that you know the meaning for the behavior. The behavior might be a fact, but the meaning of the behavior is not. Assumptions that you know why your child or partner did something is likely to create defensiveness in the other, which is likely to activate defensiveness in you as well. The opportunity for relationship repair is likely to be lost. Instead the strain on the relationship is likely to be greater.

For example, your daughter was 30 minutes late in getting home after school. As she walks through the door, you say:

> Where were you? You're late and you know how important
> it is for you to tell me when you're going to be late so I don't

worry. You spend too much time thinking about yourself and not enough time thinking about your family responsibilities. Do you want me to trust you to do the right thing or not?

Your statement was not simply about her behavior (coming home late), it included some negative assumptions (being selfish, indifferent to family responsibilities, she might not be trustworthy).

It would be better to not make assumptions about her inner life that led to her behavior:

Oh, Betsy, I'm glad you're home, because, as you know, I start worrying if you don't call. Why are you late getting home?

In the first example, Betsy most certainly would have responded defensively. In the second, she is more likely to say something like:

I'm sorry, mom! My phone lost its charge. I should have made sure it was charged before I left this morning. I know you worry, and I get that! If you didn't, I'd think you didn't love me that much. I'll be sure to keep it charged.

Or, if she did forget, she'd be less likely to get defensive and less likely to behave this way again.

I just got talking with Jackie and stopped at her house for a minute—and I guess it turned into 30. I'm really sorry mom, I need to be more careful about that. It's not fair to you.

MAKING SENSE OF THINGS: CONVERSATIONS

Conversations are an excellent activity for making sense of things. In a fully engaged, reciprocal conversation, both individuals—in this case the child and therapist—are holding together their own mind and the other's mind. As the child's notices his mind focusing on an event (he swore at his mother), he notices the therapist's mind focusing on the same event. And the therapist's mind is holding the event with an affective and reflective presence that makes it safer for the child to focus on the event. The therapist's mind is accepting the event without judgment and is not experiencing the event as being scary or due to the child being "bad." The therapist's mind remains open to what happened and remains quite regulated emotionally, enabling the child also to experience it in a regulated manner. Sensing no fear or shame directed toward the child in the therapist's mind, the child is much less likely to feel fear or shame. And then the therapist's mind—still without judgment—begins to wonder about the event. What does it mean? How was the child feeling? What was the child thinking about his mother's motives, about his own motives? How was the child making sense of the event? As the therapist discovers that the child is having difficulty answering those questions, the therapist's mind then accepts that! The therapist accepts the child's not knowing, not making sense of it, and simply moves the focus into helping the child to make sense of it. The therapist's mind is committed to being with the child—joining their two minds in the process of making sense, cocreating a story about the event, figuring out what it means.

Why would the child trust you with this process, this joint process of making sense of the event? First, the natural, rhythmic, synchronized activity of having a conversation together tends to elicit trust in the mind and heart of the other person. When both are engaged in the story in an open, nondefensive manner, trust is likely to emerge. Maybe not during the first conversation, or even the second, but with each conversation, the child's confidence is likely to rise—I can trust this person. Your engagement in the conversation includes your facial expressions, voice prosody, eye movements, and gestures, all of which say, nonverbally, "I am interested, I want to get to know you, I care about you, I don't judge you." Over time, these nonverbal communications tend to win over many mistrustful children. When they were hurt and judged by other adults, those adults did not communicate with them nonverbally in this way!

Why else would the child trust you? Because of the safe nature of your mind! Your mind is not judging her—it is accepting her. Your mind is not correcting her—it is accepting her. Your mind is not fixing her—it is accepting her. Along the way your mind is wondering with her about the event. When there is no judgment in your mind, the child's mind is able to be less judgmental. As you wonder—showing clearly that this is not a matter of the child being wrong/bad/selfish—the child becomes free to wonder a bit too. Why did she swear at her mother? The child is likely to be very sensitive to your mind as you wonder. Are you afraid of what you are discovering—are you thinking that maybe she is bad/wrong/selfish? NO! Are you thinking that the child might actually be showing a behavior that reflects a self that she should be ashamed of? NO! No fear, no shame—the child feels relief and becomes drawn by you into this new process of wondering. Why did she swear at her mom? She trusts that what you discover together will be nothing to be afraid of or ashamed of.

By now it is probably obvious that the process of making

sense is not a cognitive problem-solving process, although thinking is certainly involved in your wondering. It is not a lecture, in which your knowledge is handed down to the child, although your knowledge is certainly involved in this joint process of discovery. It is a process of gently and casually moving the focus of the conversation to envelope the "problem" so that it becomes only one aspect of this unique child. The "problem" becomes safer and less shameful when it is brought into reflective functioning. It is a process in which the features of PACE gently hold and integrate the child's and your experiences and create a deeper, more complex, joint experience. It is a process by which both of your thoughts and feelings are integrated, and the experience of the event is developed in its most complete form. Now it truly makes sense!

When conversations are developing reflective functioning, you need to constantly be aware of the need to both hold the child's attention as well as increase his desire to understand what the event means. "What's that about?" should be a frequently asked question. Curiosity comes alive, conveying varying intentions when you embed the words in nonverbal communications. Here are three ways:

1. You may want to convey a gentle, open-ended wondering that is relaxed, nonjudgmental and open to whatever you might discover. This sets the tone of the conversation so that it moves forward, being relaxed and connected, and the information explored and shared is simply helping you to be comfortable together so that it will be easier to share more important matters in the future.

2. You may want to convey a highly focused intensity that conveys anticipation and suspense, developing a sense of urgency to understand. Depending on the context, you might build curiosity by:

With eyes wide open, look to the ceiling while slapping your hands against your legs to create a beat. In the same rhythm, you say, "Wait . . . wait . . . wait . . . Did you think . . . did you think . . . that maybe your brother said that . . . said that just to make you UNHAPPY! Oh, my if that's why he did that!

[With your head buried in your hands] Ssssh . . . sssh . . . [whispering] I wonder . . . I wonder . . . if you felt all alone . . . all alone . . . and you did not want your mom to leave . . . you might have wondered if you'd ever see her again!

[With excitement, the therapist raises his arms and exclaims] That's it! . . . That's it! Your anger got SO BIG . . . SO BIG . . . because . . . because . . . it seemed to you that she did it . . . she did it just to make you mad! How much that would bother you if she did it . . . [voice much lower now] just to make you mad.

Making sense of the meaning of an event is not a rational process! It needs to be experiential if the child is to really sense that you "get it" and if the child is also to "get it." Animation, pauses, puzzled looks, all build suspense and increase the child's engagement in wondering and in making sense of something that is important. When you guess what the meaning might be and the child is deeply absorbed in your guess, they know experientially if your guess is accurate or not. Many times, you might exclaim your guess about what something means with confidence, and the child

exclaims with equal confidence, "No! That's not it!
I thought that he did it . . not to make me mad but
because he just didn't care anymore." You might worry
that when you guess, the child will passively accept
your guess as what it "really means." It is more likely
that the child will become more aware of what *they*
think it means, which may or may not be similar to
your guess. They are learning to look inside . . . and to
engage in reflective functioning themselves!

3. You may want to embed curiosity in empathy.
    Oh, how WERE you able to HANDLE that?
    Or more reflectively, simply,
    How were you able to handle that?

Expressions of empathy may help the child understand that
their experiences are important to you, you will experience them
together.

Sometimes, empathy will not encourage further disclosure
because it will invite the child to experience greater vulnerability about the experience, and they may be defending against
vulnerability. Teenagers may experience empathy as patronizing
and treating them "like a baby." You might begin exploring a
stressful event in a reflective manner and as the exploration continues gradually introduce more emotion that conveys empathy
in your voice.

Let's now walk through this sequence in a conversation that
you might have with a child who swore at his mother on Saturday. Remember that this sequence would not begin the conversation, but rather would be embedded in your overall relaxed
and connected communications. Remember, too, that when this
focus emerged, your voice would remain rhythmic and modu-
lated, your face open and receptive, you would not switch into
a stern lecture, with nonverbal problem solving expressions. It

should feel as safe to wonder about his swearing at his mother as it would be to wonder about where he went on a bike ride with his friend.

> **THERAPIST:** You two had quite an adventure! I've never gone that far into the woods there and have never seen that waterfall. Thanks for letting me know about it . . . I'm glad you had a good day because I heard that Saturday was hard. You and your mom both got a bit angry and you swore at her . . . what was going on?
>
> **LENNY:** I just wanted to go out and she said that I had to stay around the house!
>
> **THERAPIST:** Ah! You wanted to go out and she said no. It sounds like it really bothered you. What do you think made you so angry about that?
>
> **LENNY:** I think that she said no because I gave her a hard time on Wednesday when she asked me to help out in the garden. I just didn't feel like it—but I did it. She doesn't like it when I argue and don't just obey her!
>
> **THERAPIST:** Ok, so it bothered you a lot because you thought she was saying no because you gave her a hard time a few days earlier.
>
> **LENNY:** Yeah, like I have to be perfect! I can never get upset when she tells me to do something.
>
> **THERAPIST:** Ah! So it seems to you that she wants you to be perfect—to always agree with her without arguing.
>
> **LENNY:** Yeah, I have to be "a good boy" or she'll make me pay.
>
> **THERAPIST:** If that's true, Lenny, why? If she always wants you to agree with her, why would she?

LENNY: She doesn't want to be bothered with a kid who gives her headaches. She only wants to be a mom if it's easy—no problems.

THERAPIST: Ah! So, it seems to you sometimes that your mom doesn't even feel good about being your mom if you give her a hard time. That she only wants to be a mom to a "good" kid and that maybe sometimes she doesn't think that you are a good kid. And maybe not worth the headache of taking care of you.

LENNY: [Quieter now, as if he is more aware of the implications of his assumptions about his mom's actions toward him] Yeah. Sometimes I do think that I'm not good enough. That's she disappointed that she got stuck with a bad kid.

THERAPIST: Ah, Lenny, how hard that must be. How hard if you think sometimes that your mom . . . that your mom is disappointed in you . . . that she might wish that she had a different son.

LENNY: Yeah. [With sadness in his voice] Sometimes I'm not sure.

THERAPIST: [Matching the affective tone of his words] Lenny, that is hard. You do have doubts about the place you have in your mom's life, in her heart and in her mind . . . Lenny, I'd like to tell your mom that. Ok if I tell her what we just figured out—about your swearing—and see what she has to say? I can talk for you if you'd like.

LENNY: Ok.

THERAPIST: Della, Lenny really worked hard to figure out why he became so angry with you the other day. Why he swore at you. His thinking is something like this: "Mom, I'm really angry at you. It seems to me that if I argue—even a little bit—

you get all upset, and you don't forget it and you punish me forever! It seems like you're only concerned about my being 'good,' or being perfect, and that you get disappointed in me . . . disappointed in me if I cause you any headaches. That you only are happy to be my mom when I'm perfect."

DELLA: [When the therapist had seen Della alone at the onset of treatment, he had spoken with her about PACE and about ways to have a conversation in therapy with Lenny that did not involve defensiveness or explanations.] Oh, Lenny, I didn't know. No wonder you got angry with me. You thought that I was punishing you for being annoyed that you had to work in the garden on Wednesday . . . If that's what it seemed like to you . . . I can see where you'd get upset with me. Thanks so much for telling me this . . . that you think sometimes that I'm disappointed in you. That must be so hard if you think that about my feelings toward you.

THERAPIST: [Still speaking for Lenny] But you did seem to get upset at me, mom, because I really did not want to work in the garden.

DELLA: I know what you mean, Lenny. I think your arguing bothers me more than it should. I was never allowed to argue with my parents as a kid, and though I want you to be able to, sometimes it triggers some of that stuff from when I was a kid. That's about me, Lenny, I'm sorry that if felt like it was about my feelings for you.

THERAPIST: Why did you say no on Saturday, Della?

DELLA: This is embarrassing to say, but I said no because I just wanted to hang out with Lenny during the afternoon, we've not spent that much time together lately. When he swore, I got so upset so fast that I never did tell him my reason.

THERAPIST: [To Lenny] Wow! Now the whole thing makes more sense to me! It all happened so fast on Saturday that the anger got big for you both and it stopped you both from working something out—what you both wanted and how to get there in a way good for you both! Thanks, Lenny, so much for doing the hard work of figuring out what had been going on for you at the time.

LENNY: I'm sorry for swearing, mom. I didn't mean what I said.

DELLA: Thanks, Lenny, it was hard hearing that. And I'm sorry for getting so upset with you so fast that I wasn't able to figure out why you were so upset with me to swear. It feels so much better now—and gives me confidence that we can work these things out better in the future, now that we know.

Each situation in which challenging behaviors occur is unique, as is each parent and each child and each parent–child relationship. As therapists, we must start at the beginning and make sense of each unique event rather than make assumptions ourselves or quickly rely on standard behavioral management techniques.

EXAMPLES OF NEGATIVE ASSUMPTIONS AND RELATED FACTORS

In strengthening and developing children's reflective functioning, we need to be with them in conversations about what they might think, feel, want, assume, infer, perceive, remember, and value and try to develop, with them, connections to the challenges that are occurring between them and their parents. As we've stated before, this is not a rational process but rather a conversational one: developing stories, allowing our minds to wonder without judgment. Understanding the qualities of the inner lives of the child and parent will enable us to create stories that are not searching for who is right and who is wrong. The stories we want to create are descriptive of qualities that lie within the parent and child, and as these become known, the challenging situations make sense. If we can come to know these qualities without fear or shame, most likely the challenges will greatly decrease or be amenable to change. Here are some common attachment-related themes that have emerged when exploring family challenges:

The child's thoughts, feelings, assumptions about himself:

He misbehaves because he doesn't try hard enough, is lazy, is selfish.

He is not very bright; he's a failure; no one likes him.

He needs to be perfect, to be strong, and to never be vulnerable or dependent.

The child's thoughts, feelings, assumptions about his parents:

They don't care about what he wants, they don't care about him.

They want him to be perfect and mature but think he is immature.

They prefer his siblings over him; they are disappointed in him.

They don't enjoy him; their love for him is conditional.

The parents' current relationships with their child:

> The parents tend toward criticism and judgments rather than acceptance. Discipline is emphasized over other relationship qualities.
>
> The parents stress independence and are reluctant to comfort their child.
>
> The parents are struggling with depression, anxiety, angry outbursts, and/or substance abuse.
>
> The parents are struggling in their relationship with each other.
>
> There are external stressors involving jobs, living situation, moves.
>
> The parents are experiencing blocked care.
>
> The parents own attachment histories are placing extra limits and challenges on their relationships with their child.

The child's history:

> The child's infancy and preschool years involved medical trauma, abuse, or having parents with depression, substance abuse, domestic violence.
>
> The child's relationships with his biological parents involve separations and/or abandonment.
>
> The child has a disability that places stressors on the attachment with his parents.

The child's sibling has high needs that place a stress on parents' ability to meet this child's needs.

As you express curiosity about the child's behavior, you are likely to go deeper and deeper into the child's internal working models about herself, her parents, and others. Shame about herself may emerge as well as assumptions that her parents do not like her or are disappointed in her. In developing the meaning of the events, it is important not to settle for the child saying with anger that she doesn't care or that her parents don't care about her. It is important to invite the child to go under the anger, where vulnerable experiences are present. If she does not care, did she give up? Did she once care but realized that nothing changed? Did she give up with a sense of hopelessness? By now the child is likely expressing hopelessness in a voice that is quieter, discouraged, possibly tearful. If her parents do not care, how does she make sense of that? Is she not important to them? Are they disappointed in her? Do they wish they had a different child who was better than her? Is she not special to them? Again, your guide is to continue to explore the meanings of the event with an open and engaged child until you are with her in a vulnerable state where she is open to empathy and comfort from both you and her parents. Don't push the process, though. If she shows a bit of vulnerability, or doubt about her parents' motives has replaced her certainty that they did something to be mean to her, but then she does not join you in further exploring this event, give her a break and move to a lighter theme. She may go further with you into her vulnerability later if she did not feel pulled into it earlier.

When the child is on the edge of vulnerable experience and is uncertain about going further, you might invite him by leading with your voice. As your voice becomes slower, lighter, more delicate, words such as hard, discouraging, disappointing, and confusing tend to be experienced more fully within the distress that they might represent. Of course, if the child does not follow into a similar state of vulnerable experience, you need to accept that, move into a more reflective discourse about them, or move to a related or different theme.

When the child does begin to express assumptions that no one likes her, she is stupid, she is selfish, or her parents favor her sister over her, it is crucial that this experience be received by you and her parents with acceptance and empathy, not with information or reassurance. Saying to a child that of course some of the children like her—why just last week she was invited to a party—will do much less to help the child to experience that some children might like her than if you simply reply with empathy over that experience and gently explore it further with curiosity. Empathy for the child's experience is a much more therapeutic intervention than is reassurance or telling her that her experience is incomplete or even wrong.

ATTACHMENT-BASED RECOMMENDATIONS TO GIVE TO PARENTS REGARDING THEIR CHILD'S REFLECTIVE FUNCTIONING

1. Hold more interest about your child's internal working models than about their behavior (except if the behavior is an immediate threat to safety). When you focus on his inner life, your child experiences you as being interested in HIM. When you focus on his behavior, he experiences you as being interested in him being good.

2. Your interest in your child's internal working models facilitates her interest in them as well. As you explore and respond to them, she notices and becomes aware of her qualities (thoughts, feelings, desires, intentions) that evoked your responses.

3. For you to be exploring your child's inner life well, you need to be invited into it by him. During times when his inner life is off-limits, you need to accept that. He will invite you in and allow you to stay when you are tentative about what you discover there (because you experience it, that does not make it so!). You guess what you sense is his experience; he confirms or denies the validity of your guess. No arguing. He might discover that your guess was accurate later, needing time to chew on it before he could agree. And he may have forgotten that was your guess an hour before. Let it go, you don't need credit. And remember you have guesses, not facts.

4. When you do evaluate your child's behavior, be slow to assume that you know the meaning of the behavior. Be curious about what the behavior means, and if you approach the child's inner life without judgment, she might well tell you. Once she tells you, then you will be in a better position to know how to respond to the behavior, what sort of consequence—if any—is the best fit. Better to have a conversation about it than to act on your assumption. And remember, a conversation is neither an inquisition nor a lecture.

5. Accept his inner life (thoughts, feelings, wishes, intentions, ideas, perceptions, memories); do not evaluate his inner life. No exceptions. You only evaluate behavior. If you accept his inner life and wait for an invitation to visit, he is likely to explore with you what is in there—he likes the feeling of not being so alone. Experiencing your acceptance, he will be likely to share even when he is an adolescent! (Remember never to say: "You shouldn't feel that. . ." and "You shouldn't think that. . ." These are two of the most obvious examples of what to say if you want your child to *stop* sharing what he thinks and feels.)

6. Your curiosity is without judgment. You are not being curious to get the "dirt." There are no strings attached to your curiosity. You simply want to get to know her. You are fascinated by who she is and who she is becoming. Your curiosity conveys that you do not take her for granted.

7. In developing your child's reflective functioning, you need to continue to develop your own. You need to be aware of your desires, wishes, intentions, thoughts, and feelings and share many of them with your child. There are many things that parents can share with their child that do not violate boundaries or give them too much information. Reflect a bit yourself, and you'll probably get the balance right as to what to share or and what not to share.

We hope to have conveyed how an attachment-based perspective may help us achieve success with the important therapeutic goals of building trust, facilitating emotional regulation, and facilitating reflective functioning. This particular relational lens may be a good addition to many models of therapy that address these important areas of development.

chapter eight

Toward a Transforming Environment

Working with schools and communities will be a familiar feature of your work as a child mental health professional. In this chapter we outline how to share the attachment informed approach described in this book with key people in the child's life. Our intention is to help transform the child's social world in a way that supports the child's development of regulation, social cognition, and trusting relationships. Sometimes the emphasis on the importance of relationships may challenge assumptions about how children should be disciplined in schools or communities. We propose a rationale for understanding and working with this kind of resistance if it is encountered. We also discuss work with groups of parents and complementary interventions for parents in blocked care.

The DDP community has a model for this work, highlighting the role of the psychotherapy, parenting, and practice (Figure 8.1) as representing layers of intervention. This model proposes that once these layers are DDP-informed, that is when they have an emphasis on safety, regulation, and reflection in mind, the child's environment can be considered supportive of the developmental outcomes of attachment. If these features are not in place in the schools and the community that should support the child's emotional regulation, their reflective functioning, social interactions and trust in others, the work in the clinic may be less effective.

While there are dedicated and specialist DDP informed services in education settings, this chapter focuses on the realities the busy clinician faces in being able to influence the world outside the clinic. For examples of exemplar services, we recommend *Healing Relational Trauma with Attachment-Focused Interventions: Dyadic Developmental Psychotherapy with Children and Families*, by Hughes, Golding, and Hudson (2019).

Figure 8.1: DDP Practice, Parenting, and Psychotherapy

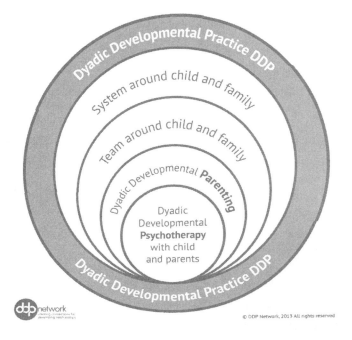

This chapter is organized around the model of DDP practice, beginning with DDP practice and its role with the systems and the team around the child and then moving into ways of using DDP with groups of parents. Much of which follows, regarding working with outside agencies and professionals, requires sharing information about the family. Therefore it is conducted with the consent of the parents and, as appropriate, the child.

DYADIC DEVELOPMENTAL PRACTICE

DDP practice encompasses the practice of DDP informed parenting and the psychotherapy. It sets the context for work with the "system" around the child and other professionals working with a family. This guides the system, the social world of the child, to consider the importance of safety, regulation and reflection into their interactions with the child. We begin with schools then move on to work with community professionals.

SCHOOL

Schooling accounts for many of the hours of a child's day. Here, the role of epistemic trust of the child will be present with the other children, the teachers, and the institution. These interactions will be guided by the child's internal working models of relationships. Through your use of the attachment informed techniques described in this book, these interactions offer you insights into their working models of relationships with the wider world. Teachers who are perceived as "mean" by the child may reflect hostile attributions and lowered epistemic trust. The presence of a favorite teacher may convey that the school is receptive to the child's needs and that it might be useful for you to work out a relationship that would offer a better chance for the development of regulation and social cognition.

The school will have its own culture of managing the challenges children present with, especially when the child's difficulties are characterized by behavioral disorders. Understanding this cultural milieu is important when anticipating whether they will be open to attachment informed principles. Schools with strict disciplinary codes and high academic expectations may underplay the value of emotional development in the child. Schools that have a balance of the two may be more open to the value of attachment-informed methods of discipline, such as working with the relationship first before the most appropriate consequences are chosen and applied. Understanding the systems of caregiving through interviews with key staff—as you might do with a parent who shows blocked care—can illuminate the culture of the school and assist you in knowing how to approach the school to support the child. For example:

- Do they find the child rewarding and can they name things they like and value in the child? (Reward system)
- Is the child sent away when they are challenging or are they brought into closeness with a preferred teacher? (Social approach system)
- Are the difficulties of the child such that they threaten the school's ethos and vision so much that they cannot see how the child may fit into their principles? (Meaning making system)
- Do they read beneath the behavior? (Child reading system)
- Are there pressures on the school that make their capacity for tolerance low, leading to statements about the child being ejected or excluded? (Executive system)

Where the school is struggling in these domains, they too may need some attention to their felt sense of safety about the child. This will typically depend on whether they have the resources to meet the child's needs, which often involves developing a good way to bring safety to the child and the school. If resources can be mobilized, the work on creating a relationally safer and more attuned environment becomes more likely. Advocating for these, based on an assessed need of the child, can be an important first step the clinician can take in creating a transforming environment. Where there are blocks to taking an attachment-informed approach with the child, it will be important to moderate your expectations for change as you approach this culture of many individuals. The role of PACE in your interactions with the people involved may be necessary if there is resistance to your approaches. Consider this scheduled telephone contact with a child's teacher:

THERAPIST: Hello, it's David, David St. Hubbins, from Child Psychology. Is this Mrs. Parker?

MRS. PARKER: Hello, yes, it is.

THERAPIST: Do you have a moment to speak?

MRS. PARKER: Mmhmm.

THERAPIST: I am calling about Fiona.

MRS. PARKER: Aha.

THERAPIST: We have been working with Fiona and her parents and I understand school is challenging. I wondered if we could share an understanding about her needs in class.

MRS. PARKER: Yes she's been quite the little handful. A disruptive influence. We call her the disruptor!

THERAPIST: It's been difficult. I wonder what makes her a handful and so disruptive?

MRS. PARKER: She fires off the other kids. As soon as I am getting her attention to refocus on task, she turns away and jibes another kid.

THERAPIST: She turns away when you are trying to teach?

MRS. PARKER: Uh huh.

THERAPIST: That sounds really difficult. And challenges your work with the whole class.

MRS. PARKER: Sure does!

THERAPIST: Fiona does turn away from people when she is corrected; that seems to be a pattern. Discipline is hard for her to accept as she doesn't seem to trust many people.

MRS. PARKER: You can say that again! She is defiant and disrespectful.

THERAPIST: I wonder what you think is happening for her when you discipline her.

MRS. PARKER: She thinks she doesn't need to listen to an old goat like me!

THERAPIST: Oh no!

MRS. PARKER: I've been teaching kids for twenty years and have not seen anything like it. She sure is rude.

THERAPIST: I wonder if this feels personal.

MRS. PARKER: She does have an attitude with me for sure.

THERAPIST: And I wonder if this makes it hard to know what to do, especially as she does it with all the other kids watching, maybe you feel unskilled despite your all your teaching experience?

MRS. PARKER: She has made me wonder whether I should be retiring! I didn't come to work to take this kind of behavior.

THERAPIST: So when she struggles to accept your ideas, it makes you feel like you are not doing a good job.

MRS. PARKER: She does! Maybe she needs a new teacher . . .

THERAPIST: Or I wonder if she needs help to see that you have a lot to offer.

MRS. PARKER: That would be a start!

THERAPIST: I wonder if we could think about how we could help her see that; help her with trusting people more . . .

MRS. PARKER: Go on.

With some PACE, the struggles and defensiveness of this teacher may have diminished and this may help her develop some curiosity and interest in the reasons behind this child's behavior, which in this case were due to a lack of trust in adults. This may have opened a new way of relating and managing Fiona's needs in the class. The mentalization and regulation of the teacher is raised and, with that, more openness to the idea of helping the child becomes possible.

There will be key people on the team around the child who will be important to work with in this way, especially if the child has difficulty experiencing the school in a trusting way:

SCHOOL COUNSELOR

Where present, the school counselor may be a useful contact to begin sharing an understanding of the needs of the child. The counselor may schedule a briefing to disseminate information and train the teaching staff. Forming a good alliance with the counselor may be particularly helpful. The school counselor may be the person the child seeks out when their attachment system is triggered by distress (i.e., they are primed to seek someone out for comfort and regulation). If the counselor is able to understand the principles used by the parents in therapy, such as PACE, connection before correction, and the two hands approach to discipline as discussed in the preceding chapters, the counselor will be a great resource to the family.

SPECIAL EDUCATION STAFF

Where children demonstrate difficulties that require more resources, working with the staff responsible for allocating resources will also be key. This may involve advocating for the child's mental health difficulties and defining the assistance they need to regulate and interact with others.

TEACHING STAFF

In primary school settings, the child is likely to interact with one or two key staff members. In high school, this number expands dramatically. The role of training and meetings, which help individuate the principles for that child, are likely to be worthy investments of time for the clinician. The Principal may also need to understand the rationale for their staff taking time to develop a different approach, which may also be one that challenges the predominant ethos.

In our work with schools, we are not asking the staff to be therapists, but to be more informed and therefore therapeutic in their approach to the child. You are bringing your attachment-informed perspective to the educational team because of its relevance in understanding this child. You are a professional, equal to—not above—the educational professionals, bringing your perspective to the professional team because it is needed to provide for the complex needs of this child. Principles regarding the child that may be relevant to the staff, shared either in training or in consultation with the team, may include:

INCREASING STRUCTURE AND SUPERVISION

Where problems with social relationships and emotional regulation are present, consider what can be done to help mediate or support resolution with a supportive adult. This will offer a more developmentally attuned context for the child to experience repair, social connection, and regulation. The discipline recommendations we provided at the end of Chapter 8 for parents are likely to be equally appropriate for educators.

PACE

If professionals understand the mechanisms for connection through PACE, they may come to understand the child and develop greater trust in the relationship. This approach emphasizes the value of delaying the sanction or correction whenever possible until after coregulating the child's emotions and making sense of the meaning of the child's behaviors. Slowing down the administration of consequences until some PACEful connection has been made is important and may include the need to address behaviors separately. Where schools feel they have failed to have an impact on the child with behavioral methods, it may be worth helping them consider it may be the timing of these consequences that reduces their effectiveness and that the child needs to be open to their good intentions just as the child must be open to her parents' good intentions for their discipline to be effective.

PROFESSIONAL SYSTEMS: SOCIAL WORKERS, COMMUNITY WORKERS, AND THE POLICE

The child, perhaps as a result of their mental health difficulties, may encounter a range of professionals in the community. Children with externalized difficulties that result in antisocial behavior may be referred to the police or community workers. Children whose behavior places them at risk of self-harm may need hospital services, where they will meet our colleagues in mental health. Children whose parents are struggling to keep them safe may meet social workers who will assist the family. Your role in consulting with these professionals is relevant and follows a similar pattern to your work with schools, albeit that there may be more work with individuals rather than groups of professionals.

Helping involved professionals have developmentally informed expectations of the child's capacity to manage their emotions is important so these other professionals can make the most effective plans and strategies about how to address the child's behavior. The child's capacity for trust with others would seem particularly pertinent here, too. Professionals who described the child as "hostile" and "resistant" will be helped if they can value the approach of first connecting with the child's view of them and the world. A shared understanding of the child's ability to demonstrate the social cognitive capacity for recognizing the feelings of others is really important where the child's behavior has led to some victimization. It may be helpful, when restorative interventions are being suggested, that the professional system understand the principles of connection before correction because the professionals will be less likely to help move the child to safety and a place of genuine remorse without this. The importance of structure and supervision, and also PACEful interactions, may help community workers and social workers "come alongside" the child to develop connection and assist the child more effectively. Consulting with these professionals regarding these principles may support the child's emerging resilience and help trust develop as they work with the child.

DYADIC DEVELOPMENTAL PARENTING

We have seen how assisting parents with principles of parenting in the clinic can be of help. This section describes when it may be helpful to run group parenting interventions that are consistent with DDP and attachment theory.

WORKING WITH FOSTER CAREGIVERS, ADOPTERS, AND RESIDENTIAL STAFF

The particular needs of fostered and adopted children have led to the development of groups based on DDP parenting approaches. The characteristics of these populations, where these problems arise, often center on attachment insecurity, with children turning away from their parents at times of attachment need. There are two manualized interventions for these caregivers: the 18-week Nurturing Attachments Training Resource (NATR; Golding, 2008) and the shorter, six-session Foundations for Attachments (FfA; Golding, 2017). The latter has been also used in residential settings. Both groups describe the principles of using PACE in parenting, help parents understand the difficulties associated with the effects of maltreatment on children's development, help parents understand blocked care, and focus on improving the reflective capacity of the parents, including understanding their own attachment history. The NATR course has been more extensively evaluated, but both show positive changes in parents.

The NATR produces positive changes in parents with regard to their confidence and mentalization capacity (Selwyn, Golding, Alper, Smith, & Hewitt, 2016). Parents reported in interviews that their own emotional regulation improved, as did their child's, and improved attunement was described (Hewitt, Gurney-Smith, & Golding, 2018). The FfA has been reported to improve knowledge about attachment theory and the challenges of parenting children with attachment insecurity among adopters, foster caregivers, and residential workers (Hughes et al., 2019). There were improvements, too, in the well-being of parents, the parents' feelings of self-efficacy, and their mentalization skills (Hughes et al., 2019). There are other benefits of being together in a facilitated setting that offers support and normalizes some of the distress and difficulties associated with parenting children who may have difficulties predominantly with attachment (Hewitt et al., 2018). The manuals offer the clinician a useful resource in working with these particular groups. These groups offer opportunities to prepare parents for DDP. Guidance has also been produced for parents embarking on DDP and these and other resources, including information for parents and children on what DDP entails, are available for free from the DDP Institute website. Stepping aside from the model of Dyadic Developmental Practice, we turn now to considering alternative but complimentary interventions for addressing blocked care.

MINDFULNESS AND BLOCKED CARE

For parents suffering from blocked care, help with cultivating better regulation of emotion can be valuable. This may help them recover their executive system and may be especially useful for in cases of acute stress, which has otherwise overwhelmed their parenting. For parents with chronic blocked care, often due to their own childhoods, more dedicated assistance may be necessary to help them manage their distress and also integrate their life's experiences to improve their mental health.

Mindfulness programs such as Mindfulness Based Cognitive Therapy (Segal, Williams, & Teasdale, 2002) or Mindfulness Based Stress Reduction (Kabat-Zinn, 1990) are good choices for recommending to parents because they are 1) short, 2) consistent with an attachment theory driven approach, and 3) evidence based. These group-based programs effectively address a wide range of emotional suffering, including recurrent depression (Teasdale et al., 2000), anxiety (Roemer, Orsillo, & Salters-Pedneault, 2008), and where mindfulness first entered Western practices, chronic pain (Kabat-Zinn, Lipworth, & Burney, 1985). Improving mindfulness in parents has been identified as a potential mechanism to improve parenting capacity by reducing the physiological arousal some parents may struggle with (Bögels, Lehtonen, & Restifo, 2010). Indeed, Baylin and Hughes (2016) describe how the executive system in the parenting system can be strengthened with mindful parenting practices. Research has shown a number of effects on the brain function of mindfulness participants, including in areas associated with emotional regulation (Chambers, Gullone, & Allen, 2009). There is a proposition too that a mindful approach in the parent may be a path toward secure attachment (Siegel & Hartzell, 2003), and mindfulness is facilitated through PACEful interactions (Hughes, 2013). But how precisely might mindfulness in a parenting context assist and compliment an attachment informed approach? If mindfulness is described as the "awareness that emerges through paying attention, on purpose, in the present moment, and nonjudgmentally to the unfolding of experience moment by moment" (Kabat-Zinn, 2003, p. 145), what constitutes mindful parenting? A model of mindful parenting has been defined by Duncan, Coatsworth, and

Greenberg (2009) as involving five dimensions and brings that alert our attention to the relevance of mindfulness to the address the parenting systems identified by the model of blocked care. Duncan, Coatsworth and Greenberg (2009) propose that mindful parenting involves:

a.   Listening with full attention
b.   Nonjudgmental acceptance of self and child
c.   Emotional awareness of self and child
d.   Self-regulation in the parenting relationship
e.   Compassion for self and child (Duncan et al., 2009)

When each of these dimensions is present we can see many of the facets associated with unblocked care and the qualities associated with secure attachment, namely, emotional regulation in the parent, a relationship focus, and child reading capacities. Duncan et al., (2009) also specify behaviors that illustrate the five dimensions in their model which, through the lens of an attachment approach, reflect the qualities of secure attachment and caregiving that is not so overwhelmed by stress. We have included some of these behaviors and paired them with the associated systems in care giving or features in the child:

• Correctly discerning the child's behavioral cues (Child reading and reflective functioning)
• Accurately perceiving the child's verbal communication (Child reading and reflective functioning)
• Reduced use and influence of cognitive constructions and expectations (Reflective functioning)
• Nonjudgmental acceptance of self and child (Acceptance in PACE)
• Emotional awareness of self and child (Executive System, Emotional Regulation)

- Responsiveness to the child's needs and emotions (Social Approach System)
- Less dismissing of the child's emotions (Social Approach System)
- Less discipline that results from parent's strong negative emotion, such as anger, disappointment, shame (Executive System)
- Self-regulation in the parenting relationship and emotion regulation in the parenting context (Executive System, Emotional Regulation)
- Parenting in accordance with goals and values (Parent Meaning Making System)
- Less negative affect displayed in the parent–child relationship (Executive System and Emotional Regulation)
- Less self-blame when parenting goals are not achieved (Executive System)

Adapted from Duncan et al. (2009)

Mindfulness groups have been applied specifically to populations, such as adoptive parents, that experience an increased risk of parenting stress, which is often associated with the attachment and mental health difficulties of their children (Harris-Waller, Granger, & Gurney-Smith, 2016). This *probably* reflects a population at greater risk of child-specific blocked care, given the increased prevalence of these difficulties. There is some evidence, too, that higher levels of mindfulness in the adoptive parent are associated with less parenting stress (albeit that the difficulites the child demonstrates is the best predictor of parenting stress) (Glossop, 2013). Indeed, the application of mindfulness in adoption has been shown to be promising (Gurney-Smith, Downing, Kidd, & McMillin, 2017). Mindfulness is also helpful for parents of children with a range of needs, including ADHD (Van der Oord, Bögels, & Peijnenburg, 2012) and mindfulness has been associated with reduced child mental health difficulties (Parent, McKee, Rough, & Forehand, 2016). Evidence-based mindfulness groups, such as Mindfulness Based Cognitive Therapy or Mindfulness Based Stress Reduction, may therefore be an excellent route to help the parent recover their capacity to manage their distress. This is relevant when their parenting is blocked by events that have overwhelmed their care-giving systems. While recommending mindfulness for a parent may need to be carefully explained, mindfulness is complimentary to an attachment informed approach and may be a useful precedent to attachment informed therapy, as described in this book. Parents with blocked care may, as we have suggested, need more help than simply assisting with their emotional regulation. The role of compassion-focused therapy may be particularly helpful here because using mindfulness and compassion exercises helps in work with parents who have troubled childhood backgrounds and, often, a pattern of resistance to help (Gilbert, 2010, for an introduction).

CONCLUSIONS

Recognizing that the "child and context are mutually transforming" (Sroufe et al., 1999, p. 2) directs our attention to the child's wider social world to support the child's resilience and development. By taking a developmental and attachment informed approach, principles that are in keeping with the origin of these difficulties can be introduced to support the work in the clinic. Embracing other interventions that compliment this approach may also offer opportunities to help parents recover their parenting abilities and by engaging the social world of the child reinforces that it does indeed take a village to raise a child.

chapter nine

Final Thoughts

Now we have shared much of what we believe is important to focus on from an attachment theory point of view, it would probably be congruent to reflect on what we have learned to help you consider the implications this might have for your practice. In this chapter we describe what you might expect from taking this approach and how both you and your clients may thrive while using this approach. We also provide some notes on how to recognize change and some pointers regarding how you may wish to use the ideas in this book alongside other models of intervention.

WHAT WE HAVE LEARNED

We would like to make sense of what you have read by distilling some of the ideas. Then we will offer some guidance about how to apply some of these ideas in your practice.

TRUST, EMOTIONAL REGULATION, AND SOCIAL COGNITION FIRST; ATTACHMENT SECOND

In our review and description of the DDP model, we emphasized the relevance of the markers of the effects of attachment security on children and their parents. From a book on attachment and mental health, the reader may have expected more focus on changing attachment styles. Instead our proposal is that using the qualities found in attachment security, may tackle the core of the difficulties for the families we see that is the developmental triad of safety and trust, regulation and reflective function. Whether attachment changes as a result needs more investigation, but suffice it to say, a developmentally-informed approach in this way to understanding mental health and how we influence it is compatible with what we know about the research and the key principles of attachment theory. By bringing the qualities known to be associated with secure attachment to our work, we are actively working on the developmental areas associated with attachment but also found to be important to mental well-being and development rather than explicitly focusing on our client's attachment experiences per se to the exclusion of other causes. This point may seem nuanced, but it is an important one to make.

RELATIONSHIP FIRST, PROBLEMS SECOND

If you are geared up for working with difficulties and problems and usually infused with an emphasis on pathology, the ideas in this book—namely, to leave these aspects aside in the early stages of working with families—may be challenging. It may challenge many of our colleagues, communities, and schools, too. We do not underestimate the importance of "getting to work," but in order to do so, we believe we need another approach, one that values relationships. For us, this is frequently the first part of "the work." We believe that time spent here is worth the investment. We also know that the human characteristics of empathy, repair, and affirmation that we have reviewed are key to effective psychotherapies with adults, and far smaller effects are associated with which treatment is chosen: "It ain't what you do, it's the way that you do it." This may be difficult for those who work in cultures where performance and outcomes are paramount. While further work looks at these aspects for children's outcomes, the rationale for attachment theory covered in this book may help justify an approach to your practice that values this emphasis on attachment theory. Indeed, you will be addressing the core symptoms of a disorder by attending to trust, regulation, and reflective functioning before a more specific problem-orientated intervention is chosen.

DEVELOPMENT *AND* PSYCHOPATHOLOGY?

Often, as we have referred to, the dominant model in mental health *is* "mental health." We seek to find pathology, to diagnose, and to treat. We know that in busy clinics, colleagues and parents may say, "Yes that's all well and good, he had a difficult start; but what is the diagnosis, and what do you propose to DO about it?" The dominant culture may not value the importance of relationships, and certainly when we are stressed, we simply want the "problem" to go away. We do not criticize this approach, as mental health disorders need good treatments. We recognize that integrating a developmental model, such as attachment theory, alongside this approach can be difficult in some cultures. Although developmental psychopathology is a field of study, bringing it to the clinic may be daunting. We hope that the emphasis on understanding attachment theory as a developmental model, which suggests paying attention to the developmental effects of attachment, is worthwhile to your client's mental health and brings both strands of "development *and* psychopathology" together.

ATTACHMENT AS A MODERATOR FOR OUTCOMES

Our premise is that alleviating mental health symptoms is more plausible and possible when we focus on developmental outcomes associated with insecure attachment (when present). To date, there are insufficient studies, to our knowledge, that look at how attachment may predict outcomes for families; this is where attachment is seen as a moderator for outcomes. There has been some early work in the adult mental health field, which is worth a look if you are considering embedding an attachment-informed approach in your practice. In the adult literature, there are some indicators that tailoring interventions to attachment style is important. Levy, Kivity, Johnson, and Gooch (2018) recently conducted a meta-analysis in this area that looked at 36 studies of therapies, such as cognitive behavioral therapy (CBT), psychodynamic psychotherapy, Emotion Focused Therapy, and Dialectical Behavioral Therapy, including one study looking at an attachment-informed approach (attachment-based family therapy). They found that the pre-treatment condition of secure attachment predicted better outcomes than a pre-treatment condition of insecure attachment. If attachment security improved in the course of therapy, so did outcome. Of note, they found some evidence that those with pre-treatment insecurity do better if the therapy focuses on interpersonal interactions and close relationships. These findings therefore support the relevance of attachment to therapy outcomes in adults. Of course, there is more to do to bring this research into the child mental health field, but these results suggest that a focus on the relationship in which insecurity is present is valid. Also, positive changes in security during therapy are associated with better outcomes (although which influences which is harder to determine), suggesting an attachment focus may benefit mental health symptoms, too.

HOW TO INTEGRATE THESE IDEAS INTO YOUR PRACTICE

We believe that the practical suggestions in this book for adopting a more attachment-informed relational approach will not detract from your established skills and practice. It may be that implementing the ideas makes it feel like you are actively humanizing your work, bringing more of yourself into the work. If this happens, it is a positive thing! We are asking you to bring your own secure features to your relationships with clients, and this may mean you value some of your own characteristics more. Again, a positive thing! You may notice you are more playful, you don't move so quickly into problem solving, you convey more empathy, you attend to how you use your voice more . . . you may notice that your clients laugh more and/or cry more than you anticipated. You may notice you are more moved by experiences, not in a troubled, unresolved way, but in a way that has promoted regulation and reflection to let those experiences pass and understanding their meaning for you and your client. What happens specifically will of course be unique to you and your clients. If you do intend to take these ideas further, talking with your clinical supervisor would be good practice and would be helpful. In taking this stance, you will also be learning from your clients and in doing so you will be keeping both you and the families firmly in a place of safety.

How does this approach fit with other models? On paper and from our own practice, we think that these ideas would be complimentary to other models, with some moments of exception.

We seek to anticipate, briefly, some of these exceptions from the predominant models around:

If your discipline is social learning theory, you may struggle with not recommending purely behavioral approaches without considering the relationship first. This is not to say that behavioral approaches are not helpful, for example, we use those principles in establishing consequences in the context of connection before correction and the two hands of discipline. Work on the relationship will come first, and a well-informed behavioral response would probably benefit the client once this is established. We also emphasize the importance of the context in which difficulties occur. Attachment theory emphasizes this in the social environment of the other—usually the parent. This extends to the community. If behavioral responses and contingencies are to be effective, we believe that they need to be delivered with an understanding of the meaning of the behavior and delivered in a context that promotes learning. The child is more likely to accept consequences, discipline, and guidance as his mistrust and shame decrease. Secure children need less help understanding that people have good intentions for them, and this may be why behavioral approaches with these children may work better. As we have outlined, children with insecure representations will demonstrate lower epistemic trust, and they are less likely to benefit from guidance.

If you have a cognitive behavioral orientation, our attachment informed approach may challenge your emphasis on thoughts first and less focus on affect. As the client begins to trust you more, become more capable of reflective functioning, and have better self-regulation, they may benefit from being able to notice their thoughts and work effectively in a cognitive behavioral way. Establishing helpful "in the moment" ways to self-regulate will be possible when the child knows their own mind (developmental expectations notwithstanding) and when they have the capacity to be coregulated. If their anxiety or depression overwhelms them and, due to mistrust, they turn away from others, their relational isolation makes it harder for them to better know their experience, to be able to explore the world, and to "test out" their assumptions about the world.

Dialectical Behavioral Therapy includes mindfulness and distress tolerance. You may need to develop the individual's capacity for self-regulation before they are able to benefit fully from these approaches. This is especially true if insecurity of attachment and associated mistrust is present.

Individual child psychotherapy may be challenged by the integrating and active participation of the parent in resolving the child struggles in relationships and their views of the world. DDP may indeed seem at a counterpoint to individual psychotherapy with children. There may be times when providing opportunities for connection with an attachment-informed therapist alone may be necessary in cases where the parents' blocked care is severe and it would not be safe to provide family sessions. However, the attachment-based perspective would encourage providing sessions with both parent and child as soon as possible, based on the rationale that where insecurity is present, the presence of the primary attachment relationships would definitely be indicated.

We hope your knowledge of your approach combined with the ideas you have gleaned from this book offer some chance for integration in your practice.

A NOTE ON MEASUREMENT OF CHANGE

Our clients' narratives give us a rich array of what changes have meaning for them. We also are probably bound, both professionally and within service parameters, to demonstrate with standard measures what changes have occurred. This reporting requires some thought, as typically the focus of measurements may be expected to demonstrate a reduction in symptoms of mental disorder rather than what positive developmental changes have occurred. So, for a developmentally informed model, how might we measure change using standard measures?

We might expect features such as trust, emotional understanding, reflective function, capacity for interactive repair, and emotional regulation to start to improve. We would also anticipate, from the research, that these improvements will have positive effects on mental disorder symptomatology. Measures of mental health disorder are not covered here. There are so many! Because our focus in this book has been on the developmental variables associated with attachment, we concentrate on evaluations that would be of potential use in these domains. These evaluations are orientated to a strengths-based assessment approach, as we are measuring developmental change. We suggest measures that we think are realistic and will not require direct testing or assessment used in research studies. However, we anticipate that measures of mental health difficulties, specific to the child's situation and the focus of your treatment model, will form part of your routine evaluations. Taking time to evaluate our work helps inform our conversations with families and our colleagues about what has been helpful and what has not worked out and why. As we do with all interventions, we value an open dialogue about this process and consider it part of safe ethical practice to do so.

HOW TO LOOK

If we are proposing changes to both parent and child, we will need to focus our attention there. In this book, we have discussed the parent first, so let's start there.

PARENTS: EMOTIONAL REGULATION AND SOCIAL COGNITION

We have emphasized that parenting stress, as a core symptom of possible blocked care, may be useful to measure. Changes in stress for the better may tell us that the parenting task has become somewhat easier, potentially more rewarding and that the parents are better regulated. The Parenting Stress Index (Abidin, 2012) is useful and well validated for parents with newborn to 12-year-old children, and it can measure stress associated with the task of parenting and pick up on external factors that may be stressful for parents. This questionnaire may also be useful when thinking about how stressful events impact on the parent. Sometimes more general measures of well-being may be helpful. For example, the Hospital and Anxiety Depression Scale (Zigmond & Snaith, 1983) is a quick and useful measure. Also the Brief Parental Self-Efficacy Scale assesses a parent's belief that they can effectively perform or manage tasks related to parenting (Child Outcomes Research Consortium; www.corc .uk.net) and may give you insights to parenting capacity.

We may wish to determine how and how much the parent's perception of their relationship with their child has changed. The Carer Questionnaire was developed by Golding & Picken (2004) and is also known as the Thinking About Your Child Questionnaire. It gives an overall measure of the parent's levels of understanding, sense of reward in the relationship, and perception of how open the child is to their parenting. It was developed for use with adoptive or foster parents but would be helpful for all parents.

Parental reflectivity may also be expected to rise. The Parental Reflective Function Scale (PRFQ; Luyten et al., 2017) measures mentalizing, using three scales, and levels of interest and curiosity in the child's mental states and has been shown to reflect change following parenting groups (e.g., Selwyn, Golding, Alper, Smith & Hewitt, 2016) .

CHILD: EMOTIONAL REGULATION AND SOCIAL COGNITION

For the child, we may expect some improvement in their capacity for regulating their emotions and their ability to be coregulated. The Behavior Rating Inventory of Executive Function (BRIEF-2; Gioia, Isquith, Guy, & Kenworthy, 2015) is a measure of executive functions suitable for children aged 5–18, which can be completed by the child (if aged 11 and over), the school, and a caregiver at home. It is comprised of three indices, including the Emotional Regulation Index, which is probably more open to changes consistent with the approach taken in DDP.

Measures of positive social behavior may be useful as a marker of change in children. The Behavioral and Emotional Rating Scale-2 (BERS-2; Buckley & Epstein, 2004) is useful for measuring social behavior, and it is suitable for school settings, looks at change in relationships, and evaluates the child's capacity to receive comfort and to trust others. There are fewer measures that do not require direct testing of social cognition, such as affect recognition and theory of mind, but these assessments are available in neuropsychological test batteries.

WHEN TO LOOK

Most clinicians will probably take advantage of their contact with the family at the end of an intervention to ask for their experience and to complete some evaluations. Often this is when any measurements take place. We would add, however, that there may be changes that the hard-working clinician might be unlikely to witness after their client leaves their office for the last time that are worth some attention here.

As the changes promoted in attachment-oriented therapy are developmental in nature, we might expect change to take time. Remember the principles of developmental theory regarding how change may occur and the railway track analogy we introduced in Chapter 2. If changes to the parent–child relationship or within the school setting are in place, results may develop even after the intervention is completed. Benefits may continue long into the child's life. If the conditions for such developmental changes are in place, then the child may be getting back toward the right track; moving away from that branch toward further mental health problems and instead negotiating life's stresses and developmental challenges better. Some children may thrive in response to positive changes in their parent's responses to them, yet some may not, as the role of differential susceptibility might predict. Deciding when to measure outcomes will therefore depend on these aspects, especially if the focus is on developmental features, such as emotional regulation or social cognitive capacities. If the attention is on disorder symptomatology, this too may show changes later on, as developmental progress becomes established to reduce their severity or their impact further down the track. Work is already underway to evaluate and research DDP robustly to help with improve our understanding of change using an attachment informed approach in development and mental health.

FINAL REMARKS

We began this book by proposing that if we utilize the qualities of human relationships, found in secure attachment, we might

begin to enhance the developmental outcomes attachment theory would predict as being important to mental health; named
here as the developmental triad of safety and trust, regulation
and reflection. We also proposed that paying attention to the
relational side of our work by actively embodying these secure
attachment features in a model which practically applies attachment theory to our interactions with clients—whatever their
specific mental health problem—may offer an enhanced way
to engage your clients with interventions developed for specific
mental health problems. These are interventions you know well
in your trainings and practice. What may have been new to
you before you read this book was the practical application
of attachment theory to your work. Our aspiration, now that
we have reached the end of the book, is that by translating
the qualities of secure attachment (safety, trust, regulation and
reflection) to your work, the potential for more human connection is possible. With more connection with your families
in your practice, we hope you will find they have better outcomes from the treatments you have to offer. By embracing an
understanding that attachment is universal to all human relationships, you can be ready to combine these qualities to your
interventions. In this way, we invite you to slow down so you
can both utilize and value these qualities, as these will be valued by your clients too, as you engage in the human endeavour
of alleviating distress and suffering from mental health problems. Both what you know and how you relate to your clients
are the instruments for change.

references

Abidin, R. R. (2012). *Parenting Stress Index,* (PSI-4). Lutz, FL: Psychological Assessment Resources.

Ainsworth, M. D. S., Blehar, M. C., & Waters, E. (1978). *Patterns of Attachment: A Psychological Study of the Strange Situation.* Hillsdale, NJ: Lawrence Erlbaum Associates.

Aldao, A., Nolen-Hoeksema, S., & Schweizer, S. (2010). Emotion-regulation strategies across psychopathology: A meta-analytic review. *Clinical Psychology Review, 30*(2), 217–237.

Alink, L. R., Cicchetti, D., Kim, J., & Rogosch, F. A. (2009). Mediating and moderating processes in the relation between maltreatment and psychopathology: Mother-child relationship quality and emotion regulation. *Journal of Abnormal Child Psychology, 37*(6), 831–843.

Baylin, J., & Hughes, D. A. (2016). *The neurobiology of attachment-focused therapy: Enhancing connection & trust in the treatment of children & adolescents (Norton Series on Interpersonal Neurobiology).* New York, NY: W. W. Norton & Company.

Beebe, B. & Lachmann, F.M. (2014). *The origins of attachment: infant research and adult treatment.* New York: Routledge.

Belsky, J., & Fearon, R. P. (2002). Early attachment security, subsequent maternal sensitivity, and later child development: Does continuity in development depend upon continuity of caregiving? *Attachment & Human Development, 4*(3), 361–387.

Bernard, K., Butzin-Dozier, Z., Rittenhouse, J., & Dozier, M. (2010). Cortisol production patterns in young children living with birth parents vs children placed in foster care following involvement of Child Protective Services. *Archives of Pediatrics & Adolescent Medicine, 164*(5), 438–443.

Bernier, A., Beauchamp, M. H., Carlson, S. M., & Lalonde, G. (2015). A secure base from which to regulate: Attachment security in toddlerhood as a predictor of executive functioning at school entry. *Developmental Psychology, 51*, 1177–1189.

Bevington, D., Fuggle, P., Fonagy, P., Target, M., & Asen, E. (2013). Innovations in practice: Adolescent mentalization-based integrative therapy (AMBIT)–a new integrated approach to working with the most hard to reach adolescents with severe complex mental health needs. *Child and Adolescent Mental Health, 18*(1), 46–51.

Bögels, S. M., Lehtonen, A., & Restifo, K. (2010). Mindful parenting in mental health care. *Mindfulness, 1*(2), 107–120.

Bowlby, J. (1973). *Attachment and loss: Separation, anxiety, and anger* (Vol. 2). New York, NY: Basic Books.

Bowlby, J. (1988). *A secure base: parent-child attachment and healthy human development*. New York, NY: Basic Books.

Brumariu, L. E., & Kerns, K. A. (2010). Parent–child attachment and internalizing symptoms in childhood and adolescence: A review of empirical findings and future directions. *Development and Psychopathology, 22*(1), 177–203.

Buckley, J. A., & Epstein, M. H. (2004). The Behavioral and Emotional Rating Scale-2 (BERS-2): Providing a comprehensive approach to strength-based assessment. *The California School Psychologist, 9*(1), 21–27.

Burks, V. S., Laird, R. D., Dodge, K. A., Pettit, G. S., & Bates, J. E. (1999). Knowledge structures, social information processing, and children's aggressive behavior. *Social Development, 8*(2), 220–236.

Calkins, S. D. (2004). Early attachment process and the development of emotional self-regulation. In R. F. Baumeister & K. D. Vohs (Eds.), *Handbook of self-regulation: Research, theory, and applications* (pp. 324–339). New York, NY: Guilford Press.

Callaghan, B. L., & Tottenham, N. (2016). The neuro-environmental loop of plasticity: A cross-species analysis of parental effects on emotion circuitry development following typical and adverse caregiving. *Neuropsychopharmacology, 41*(1), 163.

Cassidy, J., Kirsh, S. J., Scolton, K. L., & Parke, R. D. (1996). Attachment and representations of peer relationships. *Developmental Psychology, 32*(5), 892.

Cavanagh, M., Quinn, D., Duncan, D., Graham, T., & Balbuena, L. (2017). Oppositional defiant disorder is better conceptualized as a disorder of emotional regulation. *Journal of attention disorders, 21*(5), 381–389.

Chambers, R., Gullone, E., & Allen, N. B. (2009). Mindful emotion regulation: An integrative review. *Clinical Psychology Review, 29*(6), 560–572.

Cicchetti, D., Rogosch, F. A., & Toth, S. L. (2006). Fostering secure attachment in infants in maltreating families through preventive interventions. *Development and Psychopathology, 18*(3), 623–649.

Cole, P. M., Michel, M. K., & Teti, L. O. D. (1994). The development of emotion regulation and dysregulation: A clinical perspective. *Monographs of the Society for Research in Child Development, 59*(2–3), 73–102.

Corriveau, K. H., Harris, P. L., Meins, E., Fernyhough, C., Arnott, B., Elliott, L., . . . & De Rosnay, M. (2009). Young children's trust in their mother's claims: Longitudinal links with attachment security in infancy. *Child Development, 80*(3), 750–761.

Daly, A. M., Llewelyn, S., McDougall, E., & Chanen, A. M. (2010). Rupture resolution in cognitive analytic therapy for adolescents with borderline personality disorder. *Psychology and Psychotherapy: Theory, Research and Practice, 83*(3), 273–288.

DeKlyen, M., & Greenberg, M. T. (2016) Attachment and Psychopathology in Childhood. In J. C. Cassidy & P. R. Shaver (Eds.) *Handbook of attachment theory, research, and clinical applications* (pp. 639–666). New York, NY: Guilford Press.

Denham, S. A., Blair, K., Schmidt, M., & DeMulder, E. (2002). Compromised emotional competence: Seeds of violence sown early? *American Journal of Orthopsychiatry, 72*(1), 70–82.

Dozier, M., Peloso, E., Lindhiem, O., Gordon, M. K., Manni, M., Sepulveda, S., . . . & Levine, S. (2006). Developing evidence-based interventions for foster children: An example of a randomized clinical trial with infants and toddlers. *Journal of Social Issues, 62*(4), 767–785.

Duncan, L. G., Coatsworth, J. D., & Greenberg, M. T. (2009). A model of mindful parenting: Implications for parent–child relationships and prevention research. *Clinical Child and Family Psychology Review, 12*(3), 255–270.

Egyed, K., Király, I., & Gergely, G. (2013). Communicating shared knowledge in infancy. *Psychological science, 24*(7), 1348–1353.

Ellis, B. J., Boyce, W. T., Belsky, J., Bakermans-Kranenburg, M. J., & Van IJzendoorn, M. H. (2011). Differential susceptibility to the environment: An evolutionary–neurodevelopmental theory. *Development and Psychopathology, 23*(1), 7–28.

Fairchild, G., van Goozen, S. H., Stollery, S. J., Brown, J., Gardiner, J., Herbert, J., & Goodyer, I. M. (2008). Cortisol diurnal rhythm and stress reactivity in male adolescents with early-onset or adolescence-onset conduct disorder. *Biological Psychiatry, 64*(7), 599–606.

Fearon, R. P., Bakermans-Kranenburg, M. J., Van IJzendoorn, M. H., Lapsley, A. M., & Roisman, G. I. (2010). The significance of insecure attachment and disorganization in the development of children's externalizing behavior: a meta-analytic study. *Child Development, 81*(2), 435–456.

Field, T. (1994). The effects of mother's physical and emotional unavailability on emotion regulation. *Monographs of the Society for Research in Child Development, 59*(2), 208–227.

Fonagy, P., & Luyten, P. (2009). A developmental, mentalization-based approach to the understanding and treatment of borderline personality disorder. *Development and Psychopathology, 21*(4), 1355–1381.

Fonagy, P., & Target, M. (1997). Attachment and reflective function: Their role in self-organization. *Development and Psychopathology, 9*(4), 679–700.

Fonagy, P., Campbell, C., & Bateman, A. (2017). Mentalizing, attachment, and epistemic trust in group therapy. *International Journal of Group Psychotherapy, 67*(2), 176–201.

Fonagy, P., Gergely, G., & Target, M. (2007). The parent–infant dyad and the construction of the subjective self. *Journal of Child Psychology and Psychiatry, 48*(3–4), 288–328.

Fonagy, P., Steele, M., Steele, H., & Holder, J. (1997). Children securely attached in infancy perform better in belief-desire reasoning task at age five. *Child Development* .

Fonagy, P., Steele, M., Steele, H., Moran, G. S., & Higgitt, A. C. (1991).

The capacity for understanding mental states: The reflective self in parent and child and its significance for security of attachment. *Infant Mental Health Journal, 12*(3), 201–218.

George, C., Kaplan, N., & Main, M. (1996). Adult attachment interview.

Gilbert, P. (2010). An introduction to compassion focused therapy in cognitive behavior therapy. *International Journal of Cognitive Therapy, 3*(2), 97–112.

Gioia, G. A., Isquith, P. K., Guy, S. C., & Kenworthy, L. (2015). *BRIEF2: Behavior Rating Inventory of Executive Function*. Lutz, FL: Second Psychological Assessment Resources.

Glossop, A. (2013). *What is the Relationship Between Mindfulness, Self-compassion and Parenting Stress in Adoptive Parents?* Unpublished doctoral thesis. Oxford, UK: University of Oxford.

Golding, K. S. (2008). *Nurturing attachments: Supporting children who are fostered or adopted*. UK, Jessica Kingsley Publishers.

Golding, K. S. (2017). *Foundations for Attachment Training Resource: The Six-Session Programme for Parents of Traumatized Children*. UK, Jessica Kingsley Publishers.

Golding, K., & Picken, W. (2004). Group work for foster carers caring for children with complex problems. *Adoption & Fostering, 28*(1), 25–37.

Green, J., & Goldwyn, R. (2002). Annotation: attachment disorganisation and psychopathology: new findings in attachment research and their potential implications for developmental psychopathology in childhood. *Journal of Child Psychology and Psychiatry, 43*(7), 835–846.

Gurney-Smith, B., Downing, P., Kidd, K., & McMillin, R. (2017). "Minding the gap": developing mindfulness for adoption. *Adoption & Fostering, 41*(2), 110–119.

Halligan, S. L., Cooper, P. J., Fearon, P., Wheeler, S. L., Crosby, M., & Murray, L. (2013). The longitudinal development of emotion regulation capacities in children at risk for externalizing disorders. *Development and Psychopathology, 25*(2), 391–406.

Harrington, R., Peters, S., Green, J., Byford, S., Woods, J., & McGowan, R. (2000). Randomised comparison of the effectiveness and costs of community and hospital based mental health services for children with behavioural disorders. *BMJ, 321*(7268), 1047.

Harris-Waller, J., Granger, C., & Gurney-Smith, B. (2016). A comparison of parenting stress and children's internalising, externalising and attachment-related behaviour difficulties in UK adoptive and non-adoptive families. *Adoption & Fostering, 40*(4), 340–351.

Hesse, E. (2016). The adult attachment interview: protocol, method of analysis, and selected empirical studies: (1985-2015). In Handbook of attachment (3rd ed.) Cassiday, J. & Shaver, P.R. (Eds.) New York: The Guilford Press, 553–597.

Hewitt, O., Gurney-Smith, B., & Golding, K. (2018). A qualitative exploration of the experiences of adoptive parents attending "Nurturing Attachments," a dyadic developmental psychotherapy informed group. *Clinical Child Psychology and Psychiatry, 23*(3), 471–482.

Hughes, D. A. (2013). Intersubjective Mindfulness. In D. J. Siegel & M. Solomon (Eds.), *Healing Moments in Psychotherapy* (p. 17–34). New York, NY: W. W. Norton & Company.

Hughes, D. A., & Baylin, J. (2012). *Brain-based parenting: The neuroscience of caregiving for healthy attachment.* New York, NY: W. W. Norton & Company.

Hughes, D. A., Golding, K. S., & Hudson, J. (2015). Dyadic Developmental Psychotherapy (DDP): the development of the theory, practice and research base. *Adoption & Fostering, 39*(4), 356–365.

Hughes, D. A., Golding, K. S., & Hudson, J. (2019). *Healing relational trauma with attachment-focused interventions: Dyadic developmental psychotherapy with children and families.* New York, NY: W. W. Norton & Company.

Joseph, M. A., O'Connor, T. G., Briskman, J. A., Maughan, B., & Scott, S. (2014). The formation of secure new attachments by children who were maltreated: An observational study of adolescents in foster care. *Development and Psychopathology, 26*(1), 67–80.

Kabat-Zinn, J. (1990). *Full catastrophe living: Using the wisdom of your body and mind to face stress, pain, and illness.* New York, NY: Dell Publishing.

Kabat-Zinn, J. (2003). Mindfulness-based interventions in context: past, present, and future. *Clinical Psychology: Science and practice, 10*(2), 144–156.

Kabat-Zinn, J., Lipworth, L., & Burney, R. (1985). The clinical use of mindfulness meditation for the self-regulation of chronic pain. *Journal of Behavioral Medicine, 8*(2), 163–190.

Kazdin, A. E. (1997). Practitioner review: Psychosocial treatments for conduct disorder in children. *Journal of Child Psychology and Psychiatry, 38*(2), 161–178.

Levy, K. N., Kivity, Y., Johnson, B. N., & Gooch, C. V. (2018). Adult attachment as a predictor and moderator of psychotherapy outcome: A meta-analysis. *Journal of Clinical Psychology, 74*(11), 1996–2013.

Low, J. A., & Webster, L. (2016). Attention and executive functions as mediators of attachment and behavior problems. *Social Development, 25*(3), 646–664.

Luyten, P., Nijssens, L., Fonagy, P., & Mayes, L. C. (2017). Parental reflective functioning: Theory, research, and clinical applications. *The Psychoanalytic Study of the Child, 70*(1), 174–199.

Lyons-Ruth, K. & Jacobvitz, D. (2016). Attachment disorganization from infancy to adulthood. In J. Cassidy & P. R. Shaver (Eds.), *Handbook of Attachment* (3rd ed.). New York, NY: Guilford Press. 667–695.

Main, M., & Solomon, J. (1990). Procedures for identifying infants as disorganized/disoriented during the Ainsworth Strange Situation. *Attachment in the Preschool Years: Theory, Research, and Intervention, 1,* 121–160.

Mikulincer, M., & Shaver, P. R. (2012). An attachment perspective on psychopathology. *World Psychiatry, 11*(1), 11–15.

Morgan, A. B., & Lilienfeld, S. O. (2000). A meta-analytic review of the relation between antisocial behavior and neuropsychological measures of executive function. *Clinical Psychology Review, 20*(1), 113–136.

Norcross, J. C., & Wampold, B. E. (2018). A new therapy for each patient: Evidence-based relationships and responsiveness. *Journal of Clinical Psychology, 74*(11), 1889–1906.

Parent, J., McKee, L. G., Rough, J. N., & Forehand, R. (2016). The association of parent mindfulness with parenting and youth psychopathology across three developmental stages. *Journal of Abnormal Child Psychology, 44*(1), 191–202.

Pennington, B. F., & Ozonoff, S. (1996). Executive functions and developmental psychopathology. *Journal of Child Psychology and Psychiatry, 37*(1), 51–87.

Porges, S. W. (2009). The polyvagal theory: new insights into adaptive reactions of the autonomic nervous system. *Cleveland Clinic Journal of Medicine, 76*(Suppl 2), S86.

Raikes, H. A., & Thompson, R. A. (2008). Attachment security and parenting quality predict children's problem-solving, attributions, and loneliness with peers. *Attachment & Human Development, 10*(3), 319–344.

Roemer, L., Orsillo, S. M., & Salters-Pedneault, K. (2008). Efficacy of an acceptance-based behavior therapy for generalized anxiety disorder: Evaluation in a randomized controlled trial. *Journal of Consulting and Clinical Psychology, 76*(6), 1083.

Routh, C. P., Hill, J. W., Steele, H., Elliott, C. E., & Dewey, M. E. (1995). Maternal Attachment Status, Psychosocial Stressors and Problem Behaviour: Follow-Up After Parent Training Courses for Conduct Disorder. *Journal of Child Psychology and Psychiatry, 36*(7), 1179–1198.

Segal, Z. V., Williams, M. J., & Teasdale, J. D. (2002). *Mindfulness-based cognitive therapy for depression.* New York, NY: Guilford Press.

Selwyn, J., Golding, K., Alper, J., Smith, B. G., & Hewitt, O. (2016). *A quantitative and qualitative evaluation of the nurturing attachments group programme.* Newport Pagnell, UK: Adoptionplus.

Siegel, D. J. (2012). *The developing mind: How relationships and the brain interact.* New York, NY: Guildford Press.

Siegel, D. J., & Hartzell, M. (2003). *Parenting from the inside out.* New York, NY: Jeremy P. Tarcher.

Silk, J. S., Shaw, D. S., Forbes, E. E., Lane, T. L., & Kovacs, M. (2006). Maternal depression and child internalizing: The moderating role of child emotion regulation. *Journal of Clinical Child and Adolescent Psychology, 35*(1), 116–126.

Sroufe, L. A. (2013). The promise of developmental psychopathology: Past and present. *Development and Psychopathology, 25*(4pt2), 1215–1224.

Sroufe, L. A., Carlson, E. A., Levy, A. K., & Egeland, B. (1999). Implications of attachment theory for developmental psychopathology. *Development and Psychopathology, 11*(1), 1–13.

Stern, D. N. (1985). *The interpersonal world of the infant.* New York: Basic Books

Stern, D. N., Sander, L. W., Nahum, J. P., Harrison, A. M., Lyons-Ruth, K., Morgan, A. C., . . . & Tronick, E. Z. (1998). Non-interpretive mechanisms in psychoanalytic therapy: The 'something more' than interpretation. *International Journal of Psychoanalysis, 79*, **903–921.**

Stovall, K. C., & Dozier, M. (2000). The development of attachment in new relationships: Single subject analyses for 10 foster infants. *Development and Psychopathology, 12*(2), 133–156.

Stuss, D. T. (2011). Functions of the frontal lobes: Relation to executive functions. *Journal of the International Neuropsychological Society, 17*, 759–765.

Suveg, C., & Zeman, J. (2004). Emotion regulation in children with anxiety disorders. *Journal of Clinical Child and Adolescent Psychology, 33*(4), 750–759.

Tabachnick, A. R., Raby, K. L., Goldstein, A., Zajac, L., & Dozier, M. (2019). Effects of an attachment-based intervention in infancy on children's autonomic regulation during middle childhood. *Biological Psychology, 143,* 22–31.

Tangney, J. P., Baumeister, R. F., & Boone, A. L. (2004). High self-control predicts good adjustment, less pathology, better grades, and interpersonal success. *Journal of Personality, 72*(2), 271–324.

Target, M., Fonagy, P., & Shmueli-Goetz, Y. (2003). Attachment representations in school-age children: The development of the Child Attachment Interview (CAI). *Journal of Child Psychotherapy, 29*(2), 171–186.

Teasdale, J. D., Segal, Z. V., Williams, J. M. G., Ridgeway, V. A., Soulsby, J. M., & Lau, M. A. (2000). Prevention of relapse/recurrence in major depression by mindfulness-based cognitive therapy. *Journal of Consulting and Clinical Psychology, 68*(4), 615.

Thompson, R. A. (2016). Early Attachment and Later Development: Reframing the Questions. In J. C. Cassidy & P. R. Shaver (Eds.) *Handbook of attachment theory, research, and clinical applications* (pp. 330–348). New York, NY: Guilford Press.

Trevarthen, C. (2001). Intrinsic motives for companionship in understanding: their
origin, development, and significance for infant mental health. *Infant Mental health journal, 22,* 95–131.

Tronick, E. (2007). *The neurobehavioral and social-emotional development of infants and children.* New York, NY: W. W. Norton & Company.

Van der Oord, S., Bögels, S. M., & Peijnenburg, D. (2012). The effectiveness of mindfulness training for children with ADHD and mindful parenting for their parents. *Journal of Child and Family Studies, 21*(1), 139–147.

Van IJzendoorn, M. H. (1995). Adult attachment representations, parental responsiveness, and infant attachment: A meta-analysis on the predictive validity of the Adult Attachment Interview. *Psychological Bulletin, 117*(3), 387–403.

Van IJzendoorn, M. H., Goldberg, S., Kroonenberg, P. M., & Frenkel, O. J. (1992). The relative effects of maternal and child problems on the quality of attachment: A meta-analysis of attachment in clinical samples. *Child Development, 63*(4), 840–858.

Van IJzendoorn, M. H., Schuengel, C., & Bakermans-Kranenburg, M. J. (1999). Disorganized attachment in early childhood: Meta-analysis of precursors, concomitants, and sequelae. *Development and Psychopathology, 11*(2), 225–250.

Wampold, B. E. (2015). How important are the common factors in psychotherapy? An update. *World Psychiatry, 14*(3), 270–277.

Waters, S. F., Virmani, E. A., Thompson, R. A., Meyer, S., Raikes, H. A., & Jochem, R. (2010). Emotion regulation and attachment: Unpacking two constructs and their association. *Journal of Psychopathology and Behavioral Assessment, 32*(1), 37–47.

Willcutt, E. G., Doyle, A. E., Nigg, J. T., Faraone, S. V., & Pennington, B. F. (2005). Validity of the executive function theory of attention-deficit/hyperactivity disorder: a meta-analytic review. *Biological psychiatry, 57*(11), 1336–1346.

Williford, A. P., Carter, L. M. & Pianta, R. C. (2016). Attachment and School Readiness. In J. C. Cassidy & P. R. Shaver (Eds.) *Handbook of attachment theory, research, and clinical applications* (pp. 966–982). New York, NY: Guilford Press.

Wingfield, M., & Gurney-Smith, B. (2018). Adoptive parents' experiences of dyadic developmental psychotherapy. *Clinical Child Psychology and Psychiatry, 24*(4), 661–679. doi:10.1177/1359104518807737.

Zajac, L., Bookhout, M. K., Hubbard, J. A., Carlson, E. A., & Dozier, M. (2018). Attachment Disorganization in Infancy: A Developmental Precursor to Maladaptive Social Information Processing at Age 8. *Child development.* doi:10.1111/cdev.13140

Zigmond, A. S., & Snaith, R. P. (1983). The hospital anxiety and depression scale. *Acta Psychiatrica Scandinavica, 67*(6), 361–370.

index

Note: Italicized page locators refer to figures.

About the Authors

Daniel Hughes, Ph.D., is a clinical psychologist who founded and developed Dyadic Developmental Psychotherapy, a treatment for children who have experienced abuse and neglect and demonstrate ongoing problems related to attachment and trauma. This treatment occurs in a family setting when possible and the treatment model has expanded to become a general model of family treatment. He has conducted seminars and spoken at conferences throughout the U.S. and internationally. He is the author of many books and articles and is engaged in the certification of therapists in his treatment model, along with consultation to various agencies and professionals.

Ben Gurney-Smith, D. Clin.Psych, is a Consultant Clinical Psychologist with over twenty years of experience working and conducting research with children and families in mental health, secure accommodation, adoption, and fostering. He is the Clinical Lead for Adoptionplus, an innovative adoption agency providing multi-disciplinary assessment and intervention across the lifespan of adoption. He is also the Consultant at Clover Childcare Services, a residential provision for children in Norfolk, UK. He is currently the Research Coordinator for the DDP Institute and an Honorary Senior Lecturer at the University of Glasgow.